EAST ANGLIA
HERITAGE&LANDSCAPE

Overleaf:
The Lantern, Ely Cathedral, Cambridgeshire

EAST ANGLIA
HERITAGE & LANDSCAPE

Photographs by Frederick Bloemendal
Text by Francesca Barran and Alan Hollingsworth

LONDON
TOWN & COUNTY BOOKS
IAN ALLAN GROUP

First published 1988

ISBN 0 86364 037 0

Photographs © F. A. H. Bloemendal 1988

Text © Ian Allan Ltd 1988

Published by Town & County Books, Shepperton, Surrey and printed by Graphische Betiese Athesia, Bolzano

Contents

Right:
The River Yare at Reedham, Norfolk

East Anglia

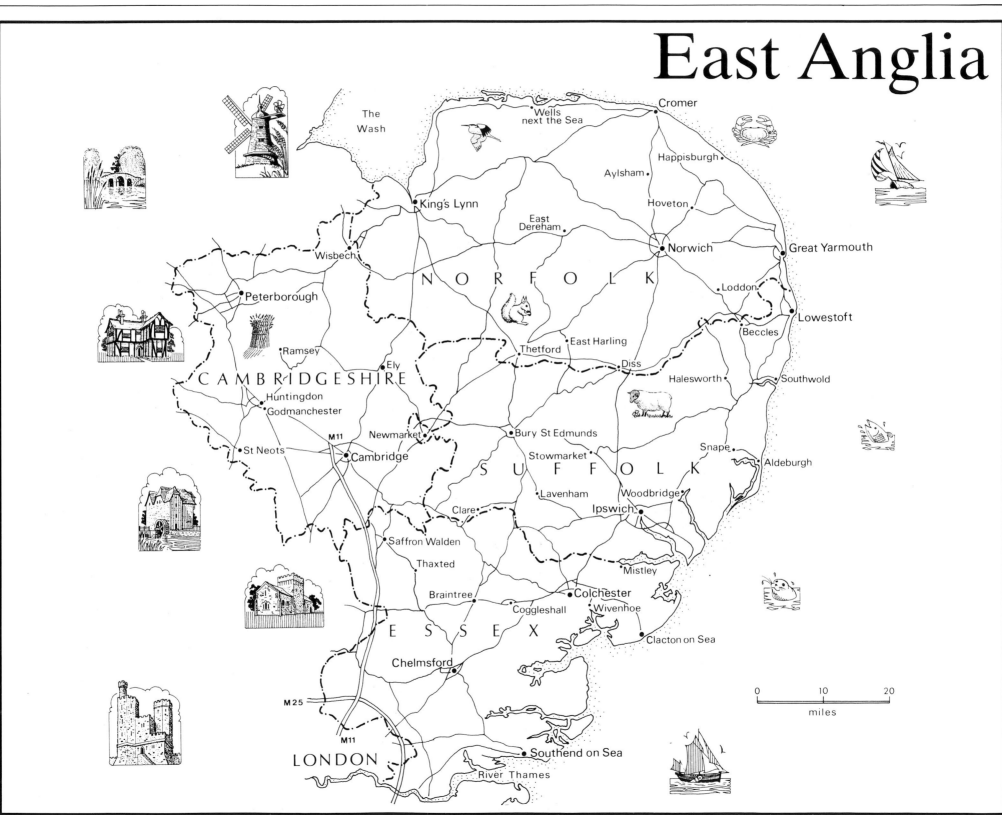

The Wash

Cromer

Wells next the Sea

Happisburgh

Aylsham

Hoveton

King's Lynn

East Dereham

Norwich

Great Yarmouth

Wisbech

N O R F O L K

Loddon

Peterborough

Lowestoft

Beccles

East Harling

Ramsey

Thetford

Diss

Halesworth

Southwold

Ely

C A M B R I D G E S H I R E

Huntingdon

Godmanchester

Bury St Edmunds

Snape

Newmarket

Aldeburgh

M11

Stowmarket

St Neots

Cambridge

S U F F O L K

Lavenham

Woodbridge

Clare

Ipswich

Saffron Walden

Thaxted

Mistley

Braintree

Colchester

Coggleshall

Wivenhoe

E S S E X

Clacton on Sea

Chelmsford

M 25

M11

0   10   20
miles

LONDON

Southend on Sea

River Thames

Introduction

Like the Netherlands with which it has so many affinities in scenery and architecture, East Anglia provides a wealth of subjects for the landscape artist. Many of the great British painters of the 18th and early 19th centuries — Suffolk's Gainsborough and Constable, Norfolk's Crome and Cotman — took their early inspiration from the Dutch school of Cuyp, Ruisdael and Hobbema but found their subjects in their own East Anglian countryside. Frederick Bloemendal is a latter-day Dutch landscape artist who paints his subjects with his camera lens, imparting to his photographs that same appeal in composition and tone which distinguished the work of his eminent countrymen centuries ago. His first collection of East Anglian photographs, *England in Cameracolour: East Anglia*, was published in 1981 and has received wide acclaim and run to many reprints. This collection, largely taken during 1986, is wider in its scope but looks rather more specifically at the heritage of stately and traditional buildings that makes up such an important a part of the East Anglian scene and adds much to its interest and colour.

The rather loose usage that is made of the term 'East Anglia' in modern media parlance makes it necessary at the outset of a book of this type to define the frontiers. We are therefore dealing with the regions that make up the English 'netherlands' — the Fens in the west and north, the heathlands and chalky lowlands of the north, east and centre and the river valleys and estuaries of the south. That this area roughly coincides with that of the modern counties of Cambridgeshire — engorged, of course, since 1974 with historic Huntingdonshire and the Soke of Peterborough — Suffolk, Norfolk and most of Essex is convenient, but what matters in the context of a book primarily about the architectural heritage is that the area has one important common factor in the almost total lack of good building stone. Stone buildings are thus largely limited to the periphery of the region, and elsewhere usually to places within easy access of waterways and to buildings of great contemporary importance — mainly of a religious or military nature until the Dissolution of the monasteries in 1539, generally secular and domestic thereafter.

But the first great heritage is the landscape itself. In almost all other areas of Britain one can say that beneath the scenery and the architecture lie the rocks — the granite, the sandstone, the slate or the limestone — which not only govern the shape of the hills and the type of vegetation but dictate the fertility of the soil, the use man can make of it and the structures he can build upon it. In East Anglia most of the rocks have either been planed flat or buried under a deep layer of surface deposit left behind by successive Ice Ages in comparatively recent geological history. What we have is a low plateau never higher than 400ft (122m) above sea level, sloping gently from west to east. The only time the underlying chalk comes near the surface is in the west where the chalk escarpment peters out near Newmarket, and other sandstones and soft rocks appear in a small area of northwest Norfolk. But the plateau of glacial deposits is by no means uniform in thickness or texture. In some places — like the cliffs of Trimingham — eight or more layers can be seen. Some deposits are clay or loam and very fertile and the basis of the extensive corn-growing areas of both Norfolk and Suffolk. In primeval times they were covered in great stands of oak and ash. Others are gravelly or sandy and make for extensive heathland. Of this heathland, the most remarkable is the Breckland around Thetford, a large area of leached-out sand and gravel surrounded by some of the most fertile land in Britain. Once virtually a windblown desert steppe, Breckland is now heavily afforested. The soft glacial deposits also account for the sea-smoothed regular sweep of the East Anglian coast from Blakeney Point to Orfordness and the ceaseless erosion of the southward longshore drift. Where that drift changes direction as it does on the north Norfolk coast from Blakeney to Hunstanton, it creates offshore salt marshes; and where it eddies at the mouths of rivers, it runs up sandspits as at Yarmouth, Lowestoft, Southwold, Aldeburgh and Felixstowe — with the biggest at Orfordness itself.

The Great Ouse and its tributaries, the Cam, the Little Ouse and the Wissey, find their slow way northwards into the Wash, but the rest of East Anglia's main rivers flow unhurriedly southeastwards to the North Sea. Perhaps the slowest are the Bure, the Thurne and the Ant that help to water Norfolk's Broads. The Waveney rises near the Little Ouse but flows 50 miles (80km) in the opposite direction to join the Yare and the sea at Yarmouth and for most of its length provides the boundary between Norfolk and Suffolk. The Suffolk-Essex boundary lies along the Stour — one of several Stour rivers in England — whose name is said to mean the most 'strong and powerful' river in East Anglia. It has its share of watermills, but when water-power was needed in the cloth industry in the 17th century, it was no match for the faster-flowing streams of the Cotswolds and the West Riding.

Another major East Anglian legacy of the Ice Ages is the great area of the Fens. As the glacier withdrew northwards, a string of melt water lakes was created from the vale of Pickering in the north through the vale of York to the Humber then southwards from the Humber to Cambridge. As they in turn drained, large areas of fenland — waterlogged land with islands of higher ground — were left behind. The East Anglian Fens were the greatest in extent stretching from south Lincolnshire down into Cambridgeshire and westwards into Norfolk. Sinuous slow rivers — the Witham, the Welland, and the Great Ouse — drained them sluggishly into the salt marshes of the Wash — the English equivalent of the Dutch Zuyder Zee. The Romans made the first attempt to drain and settle the area but it did not come into agricultural use until after 1629 when the 4th Earl of Bedford employed the services of a Dutch engineer, Cornelius Vermuyden, to drain and reclaim the land. Vermuyden

straightened out the course of the meandering Great Ouse by building two canals — the old Bedford River, 70ft (21m) wide and 21 miles (34km) long; and parallel to it, 100ft (30m) wide, the new Bedford River. Draining the Fens caused them to dry out and shrink with the result that many of the drains now stand above the surrounding land, requiring strong banks to be built, and pumps — first wind driven, then steam and nowadays diesel and electric — to be installed across the area. The result is that the Fenland is now some of Britain's richest farming land.

Two other areas are of particular interest. The first is that of the Norfolk Broads. They comprise about 20 lakes and were once believed to be of geological origin but are in fact man-made, being flooded peat-diggings of the 12th and 13th centuries. They now resemble fenland in its unreclaimed state and are a haven for wildlife, as well as people who like just 'simply messing about in boats'. The second is that of the valleys and estuaries of south Suffolk and north Essex where the glacial boulder clay plateau has been deeply incised by the rivers. The uplands are arable farms but the villages all lie in the gravelly valleys — a fact which explains the typically Suffolk landscape of Constable country, open wooded hillsides with church spires half-hidden behind them. Along the shoreline the valleys have been drowned and the silt from the rivers spreads the mudbanks far out into the shallow sea. These mudbanks are interlaced with ever-changing channels — the swatchways so beloved of East Coast yachtsmen.

Early man came to East Anglia between the glaciers, probably across the land-bridge that spanned the North Sea in early Stone Age times. Many traces of flint tools have been found and the most famous site is the flint mine known as 'Grimes' Graves' in the Breckland near Thetford. Flints are found all over East Anglia and especially in layers a few inches thick in the underlying chalk. The finest flints are known as floorstone and as at Grimes' Graves lie 40ft (12m) below the surface. Other flints are readily found among shingles and gravels. They make a major contribution to the vernacular architecture of the region.

The Romans settled extensively throughout East Anglia, building roads to link their major settlements at Colchester, Caister (near Norwich) and Durobrivae (near Peterborough) with London and Lincoln. They

Above:
Village sign at Old Hunstanton, Norfolk

Right:
The River Ouse at Hemingford Grey, Cambridgeshire

brought with them the technique of building rounded arches and of burning bricks from East Anglian clay — thin bricks more like tiles to the modern eye but very durable. Many used in later buildings have lasted for over 1,500 years. The Anglo-Saxons came after the Romans and after them the Danes, but both generally preferred building in wood to building in brick or stone; they found timber in abundance and the art of brick-making died out for a thousand years. Apart from one or two late Saxon stone churches in the stone-producing peripheral areas of Cambridgeshire, in East Anglia proper little of what they built has survived — a unique timber church in Essex, a very small cathedral in Norfolk, a few round flint church towers and the odd remnant in later churches. The main Saxon legacy is a design concept — that of the timber-built open hall house that proliferated throughout East Anglia until the 16th century and had its origins in the Saxon and Danish moot halls.

The Normans came from a stony land and built their castles, their cathedrals and their monasteries in stone where they could get it (or get it into the site) and flint and re-used Roman brick where they couldn't. Their legacy in East Anglia is impressive: the great cathedrals of Peterborough, Ely and Norwich; the great keeps of the castles at Castles Rising, Acre and Hedingham, Norwich, Bungay, Framlingham, Orford and Colchester; and the abbey ruins of Bury St Edmunds, Ramsey, Thorney, Binham, Horsham St Faith, Thetford and Walsingham.

Monastic establishments of all orders and sizes proliferated throughout East Anglia during the Middle Ages, many of them deriving the bulk of their income from sheep-farming. With their network of contacts in Europe they established a thriving export trade in raw wool, that from East Anglia going mostly to the Netherlands. And when the wool ships came back they brought not only Flemish bricks but Flemish

Left:
Binham Priory ruins, Norfolk

Right:
Maldon Quay, Essex

craftsmen — men who knew how to weave the wool staple, others who knew how to burn bricks and others still who knew how to build with them. The weavers established the East Anglian cloth industry which continued to thrive until the onset of the industrial revolution in the 18th century. The brick-makers and builders helped to change the face of English architecture — and not just in East Anglia. It was also the wool trade that gave to East Anglia the wealth in the hands of private landowners and merchants that in the 14th and 15th centuries led to the building of one of the glories of the heritage — the great wool churches of Norfolk and Suffolk, supreme examples of the English 'perpendicular' Gothic at its best.

The wool trade in the area declined because of the absence of water-power when the processes were becoming mechanised, and this caused its eventual transfer to west Yorkshire. Happily for much of East Anglia that decline coincided with the beginnings of the so-called Agricultural Revolution which in turn had its roots — literally as well as metaphorically — in the light soils of Norfolk. The great change in agriculture began with the changes in land tenure following the Dissolution of the monasteries and the transfer of land to private hands. Land became attractive as an investment not just to feudal courtiers and the aristocracy but to a growing class of merchants, lawyers and administrators — men who naturally looked for means of improving the return on their investment. In many parts of England, land was still cultivated by hand on the medieval open field strip system which offered little more than sustenance to those who tilled it. Enclosure — the creation of smaller individual fields — and mechanisation were needed if it was to become more productive. In East Anglia, and probably because of the Danish heritage, there were fewer open fields and more land held by sokemen — the forbears of the yeoman farmers of the 18th and 19th centuries — and much less disruptive enclosure was needed. East Anglia already had the turnip — the Romans had first brought it in — but it was reintroduced by Flemish merchants in the 16th century along with the bricks. With the turnip came a new form of crop rotation — 'turnips, barley, clover, wheat' — which became known as the Norfolk four-course system. It gave better crop yields and it supported more livestock and, modified to suit local

soils and conditions, it helped to bring about a transformation of British agriculture. In East Anglia, promoted by the celebrated Viscount 'Turnip' Townshend of Raynham and 'Coke of Norfolk' from Holkham in the 18th century it made East Anglia the prime agricultural region of the country, a role it has continued to hold to the present day.

Ironically perhaps, modern scientific agriculture has removed many of the enclosure hedges and filled in the ditches to make open fields of a size that would have dwarfed those of the Middle Ages.

The late 17th and early 18th centuries also brought about another revolution, that in the style of building of the bigger fashionable houses in what might be called the 'polite' sector as distinct from the traditional or 'vernacular' in both town and country. In modern parlance we might call them 'designer' houses, ones in which the services of an architect — then a new profession — were usually engaged. These architects were influenced by the steady flow of Classical ideas from the Continent and particularly by the works of the Italian architect, Andrea Palladio. Especially important influences were the designs of his English disciple and interpreter, Inigo Jones (1573-1652), whose Queen's House at Greenwich and Banqueting Hall in Whitehall early in the 17th century initiated the great change from the Gothic of the previous six centuries. What the change meant in practical terms was that the proportions of houses changed with the emphasis on the horizontal rather than the vertical. Towers and turrets, gables and battlements, all disappeared, and the great Elizabethan/Jacobean bay windows 'more glass than wall' gave way to orderly rows of rectangular sash windows. Wings and courtyards also disappeared and with them went gatehouses and great-halls. There emerged the plain squarish 'Wren' house that is to be found in towns and villages throughout the English-speaking world. Its design epitomises the Classical revolution in domestic architecture: square fronted under a hipped roof partly concealed by a parapet; two storeys set over a basement with the principal rooms being on the second floor and a dormered attic storey in the roof; a central pediment over the entrance front supported on flat pillars (pilasters); windows rectangular and larger on the second floor, most being sash from 1700 (yet another Dutch innovation); and the main door in the centre of the

Above:
Swanton Morley village sign, Norfolk

Right:
Thaxted Almhouse, Essex

Left:
Finchingfield, Essex

Right:
Priory garden, Lavenham, Suffolk

entrance front and approached by a flight of stairs, its doorcase usually having pillars or pilasters and a pediment — large door hoods were/are also a feature — and the door itself wooden and panelled. This general style — with changes to meet the demands of fashion from the 'Palladian' of the first half of the 18th century, the 'Greek Revival' which followed it, and the cheerful eccentricities of the Regency — is to be found all over East Anglia. Probably because of the large number of houses built or rebuilt during the Elizabethan and Jacobean periods, East Anglia has comparatively few large country houses of the Stuart, Georgian and Regency periods although Wimpole, Heveningham and Ickworth are among the best examples of their respective periods in the country. What it does have is a heritage of elegant Queen Anne and Georgian town houses in towns and villages, from Wisbech in the north to Newton in the south, Yarmouth in the east to Huntingdon in the west, that is without equal anywhere in the British Isles.

East Anglia's most attractive vernacular buildings, however, come from an earlier era — the wealth of timber-framed houses and cottages in Suffolk, south Norfolk and Essex. A handful may date from the 15th century but the bulk of those surviving are later than 1500 with the peak of building occurring between 1580 and 1630. After that time, oak suitable for building

was becoming increasingly scarce and expensive in East Anglia. The Fenlands had run out of oak trees by the mid-16th century and in 1604 a royal decree forbade its use for walls and window-frames in the Breckland region. Most East Anglian houses are of the box-frame type: as the name implies they were simple rectangular wooden boxes with strong posts at the corners and simple roof structures. The pointed arch type of timber construction known as 'cruck' is not found anywhere in the region, possibly again because of the Danish inheritance. One characteristic of many East Anglian timber-framed buildings is that the studs — the upright timbers — are very close together, sometimes separated only by 10in (25cm) — an indicator, perhaps, of the extravagance with sizeable timber of the late medieval and Tudor periods that contributed to the shortage of oak. The spaces between the timbers would have been filled with a basket-work of wattle — flexible twigs or reeds — which was then smothered in daub — wet clay or mud mixed with chopped straw or cow hair. This was then finished with a coat of white lime-plaster or red or yellow ochre. The timbers themselves would have been left exposed and definitely not painted black. (The magpie colours of some timber-framed buildings are a 19th century or modern aberration and are certainly out of place in East Anglia.) In the better

houses, many of the corner posts would have been carved; and particularly favourite places for carving were the barge boards on the gables and the ends of the bressumers — the horizontal beams carrying the floor joists of a projecting upper storey or jetty. Sometimes a carefully carved fascia board would be fitted along the bressumer ends. These projecting upper storeys are found in East Anglian buildings of the early Tudor period; usually on the front of a building, less frequently all round. They went out of fashion during Elizabeth I's reign — the shortage of long oak timbers may have been a factor — and remained out of favour for the next 200 years. Many were actually concealed by later generations by refronting or building out the lower wall. Also by the end of the 16th century, wattle and daub was often replaced by newly available brick known as 'brick-nogging' in which bricks were set between two timbers, often in chevron form, although in East Anglia where timbers were close together, horizontal coursing is more usual. Wattles were also replaced by laths — long flat strips of inferior timber — and these were plastered over. By the late 17th and 18th centuries, when the timber framing was also in inferior wood, it became customary to cover the whole wall in plaster and colour-wash it, usually in earth colours, buff, yellow and apricot and the odd pink.

East Anglia — especially southwest Suffolk, Cambridgeshire and parts of Essex — is also famous for a form of decoration on plaster known as 'pargeting', most of which was done in the 17th and early 18th centuries. There are two types, the incised stick and comb work with patterns impressed into the wet plaster, and the more elaborate raised ornamentation, which from simple beginnings in the early 16th century progressed to what were panels of plaster sculpture by the end of the 17th century — from simple Tudor roses to the Classical scrolls and swags of the Restoration.

A later alternative to plastering found mostly in Essex is weatherboarding — overlapping horizontal boards, the equivalent of clapboarding in North America — which was introduced when lengths of Scandinavian pine became more readily available in the 18th century. Most of it dates from the 19th century.

As the supply of good quality oak diminished, so brick came in to replace it. As we have seen, brick was first re-introduced into East Anglia as ballast in wool ships returning from Flanders and a few bricks were being used sporadically in the Colchester area by the end of the 13th century, possibly even some burnt locally. Brick did not come into general use until well into the 15th century and then only for major buildings like the gatetower of Oxburgh Hall in

Left:
Felbrigg Hall, near Cromer, Norfolk

Right:
The Windmill, Burnham Overy, Norfolk

Norfolk in 1482 and in various Cambridge colleges. Most of the known 14th century brickwork in England is to be found in Essex, Suffolk and Norfolk. As the frequent use of the crow-stepped and shaped gable indicates, many of the builders came from Flanders and probably most of the brick-makers too, burning their bricks on the site. They also introduced the use of moulded ornamental brick, a development taken up with enthusiasm in the Tudor period, particularly for turrets and chimney stacks. By the 1520s, itinerant Italian craftsmen were enriching ornamental brickwork still further by adding beautifully moulded terracotta window frames and panels as at Layer Marney Hall in Essex. Many of the motives were Classical — a first whiff in England of the coming Renaissance.

Brick did not however come into use for smaller houses in East Anglia until well into the 17th century but by 1700 it was the predominant building material. Good brick clays abound in the area and offer a variety of colours and textures. In Cambridgeshire and west Norfolk bricks are a pale yellow usually called 'white' and most East Anglian bricks tend to be pale because of the lack of iron in the soil. Reddish-brown bricks are found in eastern districts. Bricks were made in local brickyards until the end of the 19th century, but since 1880 brickmaking has increasingly been concentrated in Bedfordshire where some two-fifths of modern bricks are made, taking their name from Fletton near Peterborough. Throughout the 17th and 18th centuries, brick was used without dressing or further colour than that from the brick itself. Around 1800, however, fashion required that cheap brick should resemble expensive stone and there was widespread use of stucco and the so-called Roman cement, but all in stone colours. In more recent times even plain brick houses in East Anglia are being given coats of bright colour, presumably so as not to be outdone by the more traditional colour-washes of wood and plaster.

Flints suitable for building are found along the seashore of Norfolk and north Suffolk and in the chalk underlying northwest Norfolk and Suffolk and east Cambridgeshire. They can be used in a variety of ways, in part depending upon the value of the buildings. In their untreated cobble form, common in north Norfolk, flints show their chalky 'rind', either in what is called 'random rubble' or more carefully sized

and set in straight courses. Or they can be halved as they are in Breckland so that they show a blackish shiny face outside with the chalky cobble side embedded in the mortar — again they can be laid coursed or at random, but most coursed flint is found in the coastal areas where flints tend to be of more uniform size and shape. All flint buildings have brick (or occasionally stone) quoins (corners) and door and window surrounds which help to make for a colour contrast, although many smaller houses and cottages are whitewashed or tarred. In more elaborate buildings like some of the great wool churches and bigger houses, more advanced — and expensive — flint techniques have been employed. Flints can be squared so that the outside face looks like a small brick. They can then be used in straight courses or alternated with stone to give a chequered effect. Examples are to be found in the 15th century guildhalls of King's Lynn and Norwich. Later, squares of stone gave place to squares of red or yellow brick. But the supreme achievement of the East Anglia craftsmen in flint and stone comes with the use of flushwork. This technique originated in the 14th century and involves cutting out patterns in limestone — heraldic devices, initials, knots, tracery of all types — and mortaring it on to a flint wall and filling in the spaces with split or squared flints. By the end of the 15th century it was in widespread use on churches all over East Anglia. It was too costly for domestic use, even to the lavish taste of the early Tudors, and it is symptomatic of the extravagance of the monasteries in the late 14th century that it was the prior of St Osyth's in Essex who had his new gatehouse decorated with flushwork of the most sumptuous kind.

In some of the older buildings along the Essex and Suffolk coasts the acute shortage of building stone before the arrival of brick led to the use of nodules of a chalky clay called septaria — the name deriving from the belief that the nodules were invariably seven-sided. The Romans used them and so did the Normans for the castles at Colchester and Orford. They were used again in Tudor times but came into their own briefly in the Regency period when, ground up, they became Parker's Patent Roman Cement which was used to make stucco look like stone.

In northwest Norfolk and adjoining parts of Cambridgeshire, use is also made of a local sandstone known as 'Carstone'. It is of a coarse gritty and pebbly

Right:
Lower Raydon, Suffolk

Below:
Buoys stored at Harwich, Essex

consistency, brown in colour from its impregnation with iron oxide sometimes called ginger-bread stone. It usually comes in small pieces and is sometimes chequered with brick. It does not weather well and is usually used for farm buildings and the like. One particularly interesting use is in the stables at Houghton Hall near Fakenham.

In the middle of the East Anglian plateau in parts of south Norfolk and north Suffolk, and in Cambridgeshire, the boulder clays provided a suitable material for building in clay-lump. Clay cleared of stones and flints and mixed with straw was pressed — often trodden — into wooden moulds to make unbaked bricks and left to dry out. (This is the Spanish *adobe* technique but without the baking sunshine.) Walls were then built of these lumps, rendered and finally white-washed or colour-washed. Numerous cottages and farm buildings still survive in villages around Diss and Thetford, most of them dating from the 18th and 19th centuries. The technique differs from that of 'cob' construction in Devon where the actual walls are moulded, but it suffers from the same weakness if exposed to damp and requires, like 'cob', a 'stout hat and a good pair of shoes'. The 'stout hat' originally came in the form of a steep-pitched thatch roof with deep eaves and overhangs, and the 'shoes' were a brick or stone plinth under the walls. Where tiles have replaced thatch and modern colours adorn the plaster, it is almost impossible to tell from the outside of a street of mixed cottages which is timber-framed and which is clay-lump.

Thatch is usually regarded as being the most prevalent and traditional form of roofing for the older buildings of East Anglia, and whilst it is true in many areas of Norfolk, Suffolk, Essex and Cambridgeshire that thatch is still a familiar sight — Suffolk for example still has some 50 thatched churches — it is much less common than it was even a decade ago. The main reason is, inevitably, the cost of replacement. The usual thatching material in Norfolk and Suffolk and the Fens is the so-called Norfolk reed which grows as long as 10ft (3m) and is found in suitably wet places like the Broads. It is difficult and time-consuming to harvest and to use — hence the expense — but can be expected to last from between 50 and 60 years compared with the cheaper straw thatches with a maximum of 30, although with Norfolk reed, the sedge or straw ridge may need replacing every 25 years or so. But thatch has for a variety of reasons besides cost been giving way to other materials for centuries. Not the least was the fire risk which caused thatch to be banned in Cambridge in 1619, for example. Another factor was the pitch of the roof — thatch needs a steep roof of c50-55° — and in timber-framed houses this called for more timber at a time when timber was becoming scarce and expensive.

Plain tiles had come in as early as bricks and were widely manufactured in this country by the 14th century. They were however quite heavy and to be waterproof had to overlap three-deep. The much lighter pantiles were also another import from the Netherlands, coming in early in the 17th century as 'Flanders Tyles', and were manufactured here from about 1700 onwards. They required to overlap only once and could be laid on roofs pitched as low as 30°. On the other hand they could also be laid on the steep timbers of former thatched roofs, and thus a steep roof with pantiles is as ready an indicator of previous thatch as weatherings on chimney stacks. Pantiles are most common along the coastal areas of Suffolk and Essex, and throughout Norfolk and Cambridgeshire, especially in the Fens. Plain tiles are to be seen more often in inland Suffolk and Essex.

The pages that follow reflect Frederick Bloemendal's personal view of the East Anglian heritage as it can be seen today. It is in effect a companion volume to his earlier one in that as far as possible duplication of individual subjects has been avoided. As has been said at the beginning of this introduction, this selection looks more closely at East Anglia's splendid architectural heritage: all we as the authors have endeavoured to do is to point out what there is of interest and significance in the photographs. East Anglia also has a wondrous heritage of myth, legend and historical anecdote and we have sometimes looked through the photograph into the story behind it. For those who would know more about either the architecture or the stories, we have added a short bibliography at the end. For those who would know more still, many of the buildings are now happily in the hands of one or other of the preservation trusts and open to the public. It goes without saying that they are all well worth a visit.

Francesca Barran & Alan Hollingsworth

Cambridgeshire

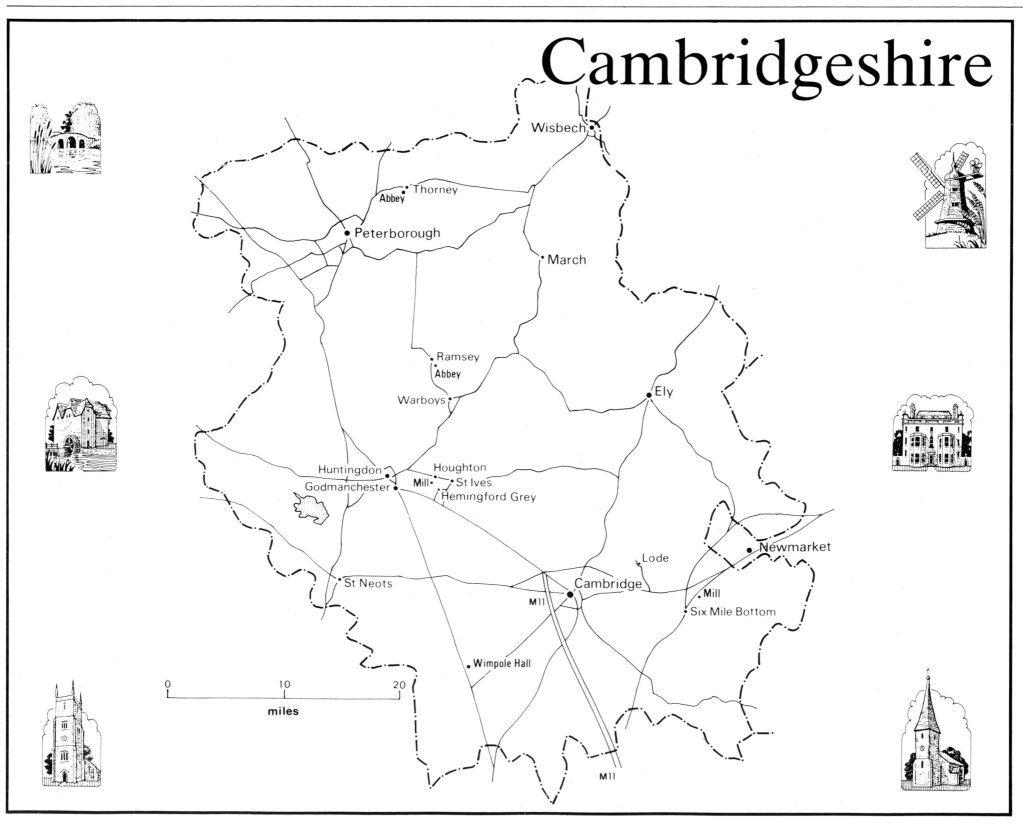

Wisbech

Thorney
Abbey

Peterborough

March

Ramsey
Abbey

Warboys

Ely

Huntingdon   Houghton
Mill   St Ives
Godmanchester   Hemingford Grey

Lode

Newmarket

St Neots

Cambridge

Mill

M11   Six Mile Bottom

Wimpole Hall

0   10   20

miles

M11

Left:

Cromwell Museum, Huntingdon, Cambridgeshire

This former Elizabethan grammar school virtually encapsulates a major part of the history of Huntingdon in a single building. It stands on the great Roman road from London to Lincoln that the Saxons later named Ermine Street; it has a Norman front which was part of the Hospital of St John the Baptist built c1160; and two of its former pupils achieved historic fame — or infamy: Oliver Cromwell, the Lord Protector, and Samuel Pepys the diarist. Cromwell was born in Huntingdon in 1599 and was baptised in All Saints Church, part of which is visible in the foreground. The son of a brewer, he became a farmer and was elected MP for Huntingdon in 1628. He died in office in 1658, and in 1661, following the restoration of the Monarchy, his body was dug up from Westminster Abbey and hanged at Tyburn. His head was removed and stuck on a spike outside Westminster Hall. Among those who witnessed the event and recorded it in his diary was Samuel Pepys, then aged 28, 'and did think it an indignity for a man so great'.

Of particular architectural interest are the rounded Romanesque arches of the doorway and the windows and arcading. The fine pillars with their decorated capitals and the multiple order arches with chevron and dogtooth decoration are typical of late Norman work of high quality. The fact that it is built of limestone — probably from Barnack — is a reminder that we are on the very periphery of East Anglia.

Right:

Godmanchester, Cambridgeshire

The name has nothing to do with either the deity or the damp northern metropolis — 'Gudmund's caester [or fort]' being its most likely origin. (Gudmund is said to have been the Danish chief with whom King Alfred made perpetual peace.) It was a Roman posting station before that and the site is one of ancient strategic importance. Two major Roman roads join here — Ermine Street (A14), linking London to Lincoln and York, and the Via Devana (A604) from Colchester to Chester — before crossing the Great Ouse at Huntingdon. The Chinese Chippendale bridge seen here was built in 1827 as part of a footpath joining the town to Port Holme, a large open meadow of over 300 acres — said to be the biggest in Europe — between Godmanchester and Huntingdon. Across the river is the Town Hall, its gables a late 19th century version of Jacobean. On its left the red brick building with the square porch is the old grammar school founded in 1559.

Left:

Buckden, Cambridgeshire

Now happily bypassed by the modern A1, Buckden was for generations a staging post on the Great North Road and still has impressive old inns in its High Street to attract the less frenetic motorist. In medieval times it was the home of the Bishops of Lincoln whose diocese stretched then from the Humber to the Thames. All that remains of their once enormous palace is visible here in the background. As is evident from the turreted and battlemented redbrick style, the buildings date mostly from the early Tudor period, c1490, and it was here that Henry VIII's divorced first wife, Katherine of Aragon, spent much of her exile. The church, probably dating from c1436, is of limestone and is of the buttressed, battlemented and pinnacled style known as perpendicular. The palace is now a school and is open to the public on Sundays.

Right:

Houghton Watermill, Cambridgeshire

This is the sort of subject that might have attracted Constable. There has been a watermill on this site for over a thousand years and old documents show that a mill and a meadow at Houghton were presented to Ramsey Abbey — about 10 miles away — by its founder in 964. It remained with the Abbey until the Dissolution in 1539 when it became Crown property, only to be sold by Charles 1 in 1625. It then remained in private hands and continued working until 1930. It was given to the National Trust in 1939 and is let by the Trust to the Youth Hostels Association. The present mill dates from the mid-17th century and it is of brick and timber construction clad with tarred weatherboarding. Originally it would have been thatched. The church in the background is St Mary's, early 14th century and built mainly of local brown stone. The tower is of an unusual shape with a limestone spire.

Left:

Ramsey Abbey Gatehouse, Cambridgeshire

Ealdorman Eolwin, a Saxon half-king of East Anglia, helped to found a Benedictine Abbey here on what was then an island in the Fens. (His mortal remains lie in a marble tomb of later medieval date which is still to be seen.) By the Middle Ages it had become one of the most important monastic houses in East Anglia. All that survives is a 13th century Lady Chapel, and the gatehouse seen here dates from c1500 when it was rebuilt by Sir Henry Cromwell using medieval masonry. It is in the ornate 'perpendicular' style of the period with panelled buttresses and quatrefoil friezes. After the Dissolution it became a stone quarry for the building of a later Cromwell house at Hinchingbrooke and for Caius College, Cambridge. The gatehouse was given to the National Trust in 1952.

Right:

Hemingford Grey, Cambridgeshire

A picturesque backwater of the Great Ouse whose delicate charm even midwinter's snows do not diminish, Hemingford Grey has attracted artists for generations. It was particularly popular in the romantic era of the late Victorian period when jolly cardinals and cheery monks were all the rage. It was then that local artist Dendy Sadler produced his 'Thursday' and 'Friday' paintings of jovial friars fishing in the Ouse one day and feasting on the result the next — paintings now coming back into favour.

The church in the background is St James's, mostly medieval but with parts which are of the Norman period. The truncated west tower is in the pinnacled perpendicular style, although its upper half was blown away in a hurricane in 1741 and is said still to lie on the river bed.

Not visible here is a 12th century moated manor house said to be the oldest inhabited house in England.

Left:

Ely Cathedral, Cambridgeshire

Ely was once an island set in the midst of an almost impassable fen and as such provided an ideal sanctuary for the last Saxons under the great folk hero Hereward the Wake to hold out against the Norman invaders. The strongpoint was Ely Abbey which was founded c672 by St Etheldreda — or St Audrey — the most revered of the Saxon female saints. The Saxons made their peace in 1071 and, as was their wont, in 1083 the Normans began building a mighty cathedral on the abbey site to house St Etheldreda's remains. Of that building, the enormous nave — 208ft (64m) long — and the transepts have survived. The choir was rebuilt c1252 to provide a more fitting shrine for the saint but in 1322 the Norman central tower collapsed 'with such a shock and so great a tumult, that it was thought an earthquake had taken place'. The new tower that was then built was a work of true genius and is unique in English medieval architecture. Believed to be the concept of Alan of Walsingham, the cathedral's sacrist, it involved building a stone octagonal tower over the whole width of the nave, aisles and transepts, and mounting upon it a gigantic octagonal lantern, a wooden tower suspended 94ft (31m) above the pavement. The result is a lantern that dominates the open skyline of the Fens and illuminates the interior of the cathedral, as Arthur Mee puts it 'like a poem in wood and stone'.

Right:

The Manor House, Warboys, Cambridgeshire

An early manor house refronted in the 17th century when the Dutch influence on English domestic architecture was at its height. Warboys itself is a large fenland village renowned mainly as the venue for a notorious Elizabethan witch-hunt. In November 1589 an 80-year-old woman, Alice Samuel, called upon a neighbour whose child was ill with a mysterious form of hysterical fit. The child took a violent dislike to Alice and accused her of being a witch. Later, when the child's four sisters were similarly affected, the witchcraft charge was repeated. Mrs Samuel was also personally accused of witchcraft by Lady Cromwell, aunt of the future Lord Protector, who promptly became ill and later died. Mrs Samuel, her husband and her daughter were arrested, tried in Huntingdon in April 1593, found guilty and hanged.

Left:

The Bridge and Chapel of St Ledger, St Ives, Cambridgeshire

St Ives is the last town on the Great Ouse before the river runs into the Fens, and takes its name from that of a 10th century Persian missionary who found his way to England and converted the local heathen. (No relation, incidentally, to the other St Ives in Cornwall — she was a delicate maiden who floated across from Ireland on a shamrock leaf.) The bridge here was mostly built c1415 but two of its arches and the brick parapet were added in the 18th century. The chapel of St Ledger — a seventh century French martyr — is one of only seven bridge chapels still standing in England. Such chapels served several purposes: at a time when travel was highly hazardous they provided a place where departing travellers could pray for a safe return and those returning give thanks, and in both cases their offerings helped to pay for the upkeep of the bridge. Oliver Cromwell farmed on the other side of the river and would have used this bridge regularly — whether he used the chapel is not recorded — but St Ives, unlike his birthplace, Huntingdon, at least boasts a statue of him.

Right:

West Front, Peterborough Cathedral, Cambridgeshire

The other great fenland cathedral is at Peterborough and it is said that the one can be seen from the tower of the other across the 35 miles (58km) of level land. Like Ely, Peterborough Cathedral was originally a Saxon Benedictine monastery church, taken over by the Normans — and in consequence sacked by Hereward the Wake in 1070 — but it remained a monastery until the Dissolution, when, in 1541, Henry VIII gave it cathedral status. Whereas Ely's great pride is its lantern, Peterborough's is its west front which is accepted as being without equal in any medieval Gothic church in Europe. It was built c1200-15 in front of the older Norman Romanesque front and it is a gigantic porch rather than a façade, comprising an open arcade of three colossal 'Early English' Gothic arches carried on clustered piers and flanked by sturdy square towers topped by stone spires which serve as buttresses. The narrower central arch spans the nave, the outer arches the transepts. (The smaller porch in the middle was added c1370 in the later perpendicular Gothic style.) The construction of the front has been described as the work of an architectural genius whose identity is known, alas, only to the God whom he sought to serve.

Left:

Mill near Six Mile Bottom, Cambridgeshire

Two features commonly found in all parts of the countryside of East Anglia are large fields of yellow rape and windmills. Rape is a leafy plant of the cabbage family which, like mustard, is grown chiefly as an autumn or winter forage crop for cattle and sheep. There are several varieties with flowering times varying from April to August. One variety, oilseed rape, is a useful EEC cash crop and is grown for its seeds, which when crushed produce an edible oil used in cooking and for margarine.

The windmill here is a post mill — the body of the mill, its sails and machinery rotate around a central post — which is said to date from 1766. It was moved to this site beside the A11 between Stump Cross and Newmarket in 1846.

Right:

St Mary & St Botolph, Thorney, Cambridgeshire

The name 'Thorney' means an island covered in thorn bushes and England boasts many of them (Westminster, for example), but this one is an island only 15ft (5m) above sea level and once the only dry place for miles around. Inevitably, Saxon monks found it and built on it c662, the Danes then sacked their abbey, and it was rebuilt c972, only to be sacked again when Hereward fought the Normans. The Normans rebuilt the abbey on a much grander scale and it became in the Middle Ages 'a very paradise, bearing trees'. (The trees included apples and vines.) At the Dissolution the abbey church became a quarry and its stones were used to build, it is said, the new chapel at Corpus Christi in Cambridge. A century later, in 1638, when the Earl of Bedford began the reclamation of the Fens, he also had the abbey church restored as the parish church of the village which is part of the Bedford estate. The west front seen here is a composite structure: the corner towers are 12th century Norman, the window and the battlemented upper turrets are 15th century 'perpendicular' Gothic and the frieze probably dates from the 17th century.

Left:

North Brink, Wisbech, Cambridgeshire

From its name and its setting, it might be in Holland but it is, as Nikolaus Pevsner says, 'one of the most perfect Georgian streets in England'. Wisbech has been a seaport since ancient times and at one time it was close to the mouth of the fenland River Nene. It has long prospered from the reclamation of the marshland and the canalising of its rivers even though the sea is now 12 miles away. As this splendid row of merchants' houses shows, Wisbech was particularly prosperous in the 18th century. The jewel in this particular crown is Peckover House at the left of the terrace. The Peckovers were East Anglian Quakers who came into prosperity and prominence in the mid-18th century and purchased Peckover House which had been built in 1722. Its exterior has the simple but imposing elegance of the period stemming from the Classical proportions of its façade — three storeys, five bays wide under a panelled parapet — and the texture of its brickwork — East Anglian yellow brick with red brick dressings. This simple exterior conceals a wealth of elaborate interior decoration in plaster and wood in the tradition of the best of 18th century craftsmanship. The house is now owned by the National Trust and is open to the public. In the middle of the terrace is No 11, an early 18th century warehouse. The bow-windowed houses are late 18th century and the stone-fronted house dates from c1750.

Right:

Wimpole Hall, Cambridgeshire

A spectacular country house in the Classical style, largely built at a time when the great emphasis was placed on making a house and its setting look like a landscape painting by Claude Lorraine, Wimpole Hall was built in several stages. The original house, now hidden behind a later façade, was begun in 1640. The house was extended between 1689 and 1710 and again in 1719-21 when the architect was James Gibbs (his masterpiece is St Martin in the Fields in Trafalgar Square), who added a chapel and a front garden. Other architects who worked at various times on the house were Henry Flitcroft in 1742-45, Sir James Thornhill in 1724 and Sir John Soane c1793. The 'picturesque' setting of the house was elaborated over the years by Sanderson Miller who built the ruin of a sham castle in the grounds c1772, Lancelot 'Capability' Brown who among other things from 1767 to 1773 built serpentine fish ponds, and Humphrey Repton from 1801-09. The house was given to the National Trust in 1978 and is open to the public.

Left:
Clare College Bridge, Cambridge

The River Cam meanders through Cambridge behind the ancient college buildings and is crossed by numerous historic bridges to make 'The Backs' one of the most celebrated charms of the university city. As that great traveller Arthur Mee puts it, '. . . in all our tour of England, there has been nothing to equal the picture of Cambridge as we glide in a boat along the River Cam or as we saunter at the Backs . . . to be lost deep in the beauty of an age that has passed away'. As here, undergraduates and others have been performing stunts in punts for generations.

Clare College was first founded as University Hall in 1326 and refounded in 1346 by Elizabeth de Burgh of Clare from whom it has since taken its name. The bridge dates from 1639-40 and was built by Thomas Grumbold in what was then the new Classical style — the first in Cambridge.

Right:
The Church of the Holy Sepulchre, Cambridge

Cambridge was an historic city even before the first college — Peterhouse — was founded in 1284, and this rare round church dates back to c1130. Such round churches had their origins in the Holy Land and were usually built by crusading religious orders like the Knights Templar whose task was to guard the holy places. This one was built by the Fraternity of the Holy Sepulchre. The rounded arches of the doorway and window openings, the colonnetes, the scalloped capitals and the zig-zag decoration all suggest the correct Norman period but, as Nikolaus Pevsner points out, the Victorians carried out a vigorous restoration in 1841 and it is said 'there is not one old stone left'.

Left:

Trinity College, Cambridge

King's Hall, founded in 1336 by Edward III, was refounded by Henry VIII as Trinity College in 1546. The new foundation also absorbed Michaelhouse and a number of other hostels, and at first made use of existing buildings. It was transformed during the time of Dr Thomas Neville, who was Master between 1593 and 1615. He built Trinity's celebrated Great Court, said to be the most spacious in the world, retaining several older buildings as part of his grand design; one of them was the Great Gate, seen here, which faces on to Trinity Street and leads into the Great Court. It first began building c1490 and thereafter was built rather slowly and in stages. The gates themselves were paid for in 1522 but the upper storey was not begun until 1528 when probably the flanking towers were built. It is mainly of brick with stone quoins although the first front is of limestone. Over the main archway is a carved frieze carrying the arms of Edward III and his six sons. Above that in a canopied niche is an unflattering statue of Henry VIII — not completed until 1615, safely after his death.

Right:

Lode Water Mill, Anglesey Abbey, Lode, Cambridgeshire

Lode is the Old English name for watercourse — in this case, a drain from the River Cam leading into the Fens called Bottisham Lode. This water mill, which still grinds corn, has been renovated in recent times and like most others in East Anglia occupies an ancient site. This area was once monastic land — that of Anglesey Priory, later called 'Abbey' for reasons of prestige when it became a private house after the Dissolution. At various times it was owned by two distinguished Englishmen best summarised as 'Hobson the Choice' and 'Downing of the Street'. More recently it was owned by Lord Fairhaven, a wealthy patron of the arts who between 1926 and 1966 created a remarkable house and even more remarkable garden. It is now in the hands of the National Trust and is open to the public.

Left:

The Senate House, Cambridge

By the time the Senate House came to be built in 1722-30, an austere form of classical architecture known as Palladianism (after the Italian architect Andrea Palladio, d1580), but owing much to Inigo Jones, was coming into vogue. The architect, James Gibbs, had been a disciple of Sir Christopher Wren and his design is an elegant blend of the Wren tradition and the Palladian ideas (see also Wimpole Hall). Of interest are the tall pilasters with Corinthian capitals which become attached columns in the centre three bays and support the pediment which is set forward. Notice too how the window pediments alternate between segmental and triangular.

Norfolk

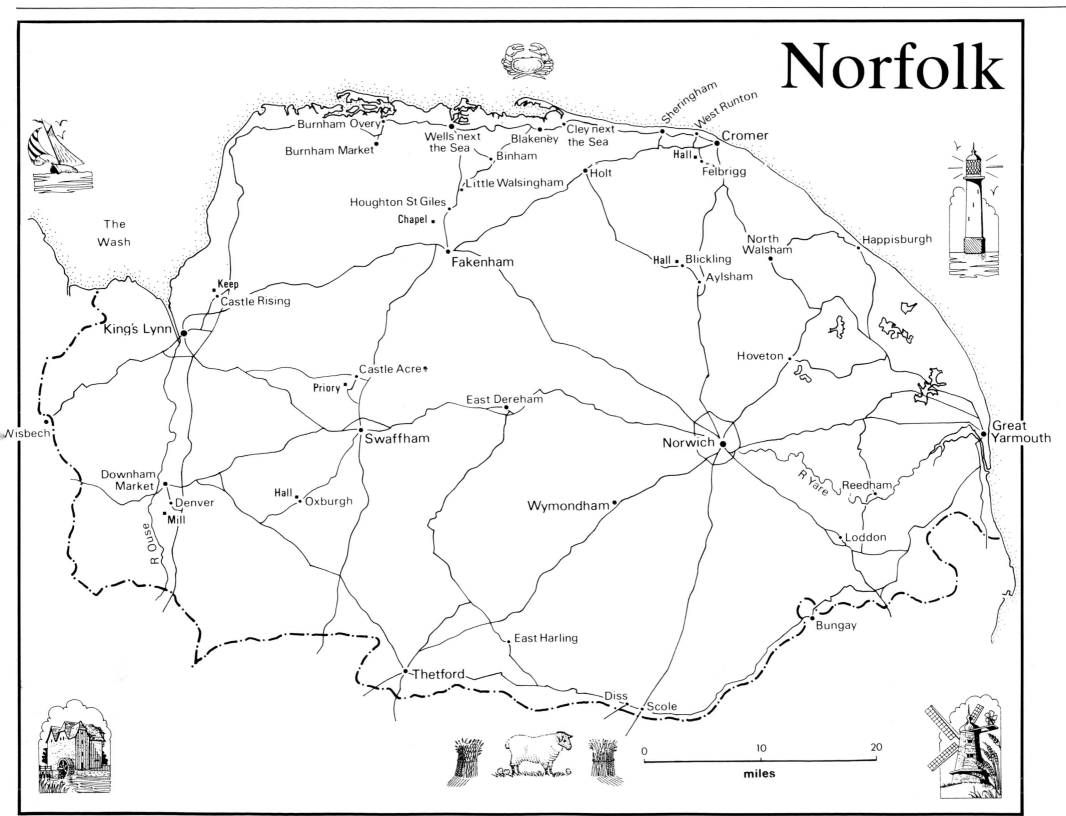

The Wash

Burnham Overy
Burnham Market
Wells next the Sea
Binham
Blakeney
Cley next the Sea
Sheringham
West Runton
Cromer
Hall
Felbrigg
Little Walsingham
Holt
Houghton St Giles
Chapel
North Walsham
Happisburgh
Fakenham
Hall
Blickling
Aylsham
Keep
Castle Rising
King's Lynn
Hoveton
Castle Acre
Priory
East Dereham
Wisbech
Swaffham
Norwich
Great Yarmouth
Downham Market
Denver
Mill
Hall
Oxburgh
Wymondham
R Yare
Reedham
Loddon
R Ouse
Bungay
East Harling
Thetford
Diss
Scole

0   10   20

miles

Left:
Greyfriars Tower, King's Lynn, Norfolk

King's Lynn is the third largest town in Norfolk and was for centuries the gateway to the Midlands for trade with the Netherlands and the Baltic. King John gave it its first charter in 1205 when it was then known as Lynn Episcopi — Bishop's Lynn — and it was from here that the same king left in 1216 on the journey across the Wash on which he lost his baggage. It became King's Lynn — or Lynn Regis — after the Dissolution in 1539, when Henry VIII helped himself to the many monastic properties and granted the town a new charter. Not surprisingly, it stayed loyal to the king during the Civil War and was the only town in Norfolk to be besieged by the Roundheads.

Few of the once extensive monastic buildings have survived apart from this sizeable fragment of what was originally part of the Greyfriars convent founded c1230. It is hexagonal and stands above the crossing between the nave and chancel of the abbey church. It is built of brick with stone dressings and is in the perpendicular style of the late 14th century. It is now surrounded by a public garden.

Right:
St Margaret's Church, King's Lynn, Norfolk

King's Lynn parish church is unusual in having two west towers and is a huge church 235ft (77m) long and built of limestone. The church is mainly Norman but the towers date from the middle of the 16th century. And King's Lynn itself is unusual in that it has two great churches (St Nicholas is the other), two market places — Saturday Market and Tuesday Market are associated with them — and two guildhalls, one of which is visible on the left of the photograph.

Left:

Old Jail and Guildhall, King's Lynn, Norfolk

An interesting contrast in architectural styles and building materials is provided in this view of four of King's Lynn's most important buildings. In the foreground is part of one of the west towers of St Margaret's Church, built c1150 of white limestone probably from Barnack. Notice the shafting of the buttress and the intersecting blank arcading in the round-arched Norman style. On the left of St Margaret's is the former Jail, now a museum housing the town's historic civic regalia. It was built in 1784 in grey brick in the Classical style complete with pedimented doorway in rusticated stone, a barred lunette window and a panel with the chains and gyves of a more robust era of crime prevention. To the left of the jail is the gabled front of the Guildhall built for the Guild of the Holy Trinity — a fraternity of merchants — in 1421. Its front is a chequer pattern of stone and knapped and squared flint — one of the best examples in East Anglia. The hall window is perpendicular Gothic. To the left of the Guildhall, and also faced with flint chequerwork, is an Elizabethan addition complete with curved gable, cartouche and pointed polygonal angle buttresses.

Right:

Hampton Court, King's Lynn, Norfolk

Hampton Court takes its name from that of a local 17th century merchant — no connection with the old firm on the Thames except that it is probably of a similar date, early 16th century. It carries the mark of the builder on the spandrel of the door. King's Lynn, which unlike most of East Anglia stood for the king in the Civil War, was besieged by the Parliamentarians in 1643 and there is on view a cannon ball said to have been fired at the time. Some of the windows are clearly of a later date and the red ochre smothering everything is a recent affectation.

The Keep, Castle Rising, Norfolk

Standing within an immense oval earth rampart with a deep outer ditch which may have Roman or earlier origins, this Norman keep was built about 1150 by William de Albini, who married Henry I's widow. It is of the 'hall-keep' type like that at Norwich and Colchester and is one of the largest and most decorated in England. The walls are over 8ft (2.6m) thick and strengthened by buttresses. As is usual in hall-keeps, there are only two storeys. The ground floor is windowless and inaccessible from outside and has a two-roomed vaulted undercroft above the dungeon. The second floor has the windows and holds the great hall and smaller rooms including the chapel. The keep was altered in Tudor times when it belonged to Thomas Howard, Duke of Norfolk. Legend has it that Queen Isabella went insane when imprisoned in the keep for her complicity in the murder of her husband, Edward II, in 1327, and her screams are still sometimes heard. Castle Rising is now owned by English Heritage and is open to the public.

Right:
Denver Windmill, Denver, Norfolk

The village of Denver is best known as the site of Denver sluices which control the waters of the Great Ouse and the vast network of dykes and drains feeding into it. Much of it was installed in the 17th century, some in 19th century, and a main outlet, Cut Off and Main Channels as recently as the 1960s. Upon these sluices depends the security of thousands of square miles of the Fens and its rich farmlands. The windmill seen here is not however a wind pump — most are electrical nowadays — but a good old-fashioned windmill of the tower type where only the cap revolves. It grinds corn.

Left:
The Priory, Castle Acre, Norfolk

The Cluniac Order, a reformed offshoot of the Benedictines, was first brought to Lewes in Sussex from Cluny by William de Warenne, first Earl of Sussex, just after the Conquest. In 1090 the second Earl founded the Cluniac house at Castle Acre. The number of monks probably never exceeded 30 but Cluniacs lived well and the impressive size and style of this priory is evidence of their wealth and ostentation. On the left and particularly impressive is the west front (c1140-50) of the priory church with its massive west window and its excess of decorative blind arcading, all built in limestone. To the right of the church is the Prior's House built about 1500, shortly before the Dissolution and at a time when the population of the priory was only about 11 and its excessive life-style had become a scandal. It has projecting wings like any other manor house of the day. The porch wing — stone and flint with chequered flushwork under a timber-framed gable — is on the right; the building to its left with the oriel window and the stepped gable is the north wing. The priory is now in the hands of English Heritage and is open to the public.

Right:
Cromer, Norfolk

Cromer came early to prominence as a seaside resort — in her novel *Emma* (1816), Jane Austen has one of her characters report that 'Perry was a week in Cromer once, and he holds it to be the best of all the sea-bathing places'. It probably became a watering place at the end of the 18th century and it flourished with the coming of the railways and possesses all the appurtenances of a 'real' 19th century seaside resort — pier, promenade (seen here on the right) and lots of shops and amusements. It also has a charming location, a splendid beach and its crabs have a national reputation. Architecturally it boasts the impressive medieval church of St Peter & St Paul which dominates the town from the cliff-top and an interesting selection of Regency and Victorian buildings.

Left:

Oxburgh Hall, Norfolk

Sir Edmund Bedingfield built this house in 1482 at a time when the dynastic civil war between York and Lancaster was as yet unsettled, unrest was widespread and some domestic fortification was necessary. Surrounded by the moat, the house is built around a courtyard entered through the great gatehouse, seen here on the left, which Nikolaus Pevsner has described as the most prominent English brick gatehouse of the 15th century. It is seven storeys high, battlemented and also has machicolations — holes to pour boiling oil, etc, upon the heads of attackers. The great hall and other parts of the house were demolished by a later Bedingfield in 1775 but restored during the early Victorian Gothic era although the gatehouse was spared. The Bedingfield family still lives in Oxburgh Hall which now belongs to the National Trust and is open to the public.

Right:

The Slipper Chapel, Houghton St Giles, Norfolk

A mile to the southwest of Little Walsingham is this slipper chapel, so called because the more devout pilgrims removed their shoes here and walked barefoot to the shrine. Built in the 14th century, it was in use as a farm cottage from the Dissolution until the end of the 19th century. It was later restored as a Roman Catholic shrine and opened for worship in 1934.

Left:

Common Place, Little Walsingham, Norfolk

As things tend to be ordered in Norfolk, Little Walsingham is bigger than Great Walsingham and is also the location of the shrine to Our Lady of Walsingham, which has given fame to its name. It is usually a quiet village, containing this small square with its 16th century brick and stone conduit (a pump house) with its iron cresset, a primitive street light. The massive 15th century gatehouse on the right is the entrance to the former priory now known as the abbey and the actual site of the original shrine. The cult of the Our Lady of Walsingham originated with a vision of the Virgin Mary in 1061 being seen by the wife of a Norman knight, Lady Richeldis. An Augustinian priory was founded in 1153 and became one of the most popular places of pilgrimage in England throughout the Middle Ages. Kings visited it, including Henry VIII (it is said), but at the Dissolution it was destroyed and the shrine's statue burnt at Smithfield. The cult was revived in 1921 and an Anglican church was built near the precinct wall of the priory. The shrine still attracts thousands of pilgrims every year.

Right:

Cley-next-the-Sea, Norfolk

Whereas on the east coast of Norfolk, erosion of the coastline is a problem, on parts of the north coast the reverse is true. Cley — it rhymes with sky — harbour is now more than a mile from the sea, embanking during the 17th century having led to its decline. Its ancient church, marking an earlier site, is even further inland. The village is mainly built of flint rubble with red brick dressing and the pantile roof usual to this area. Dominating both the village and the surrounding marshes is this tower windmill — only the cap turns — which was built in 1713.

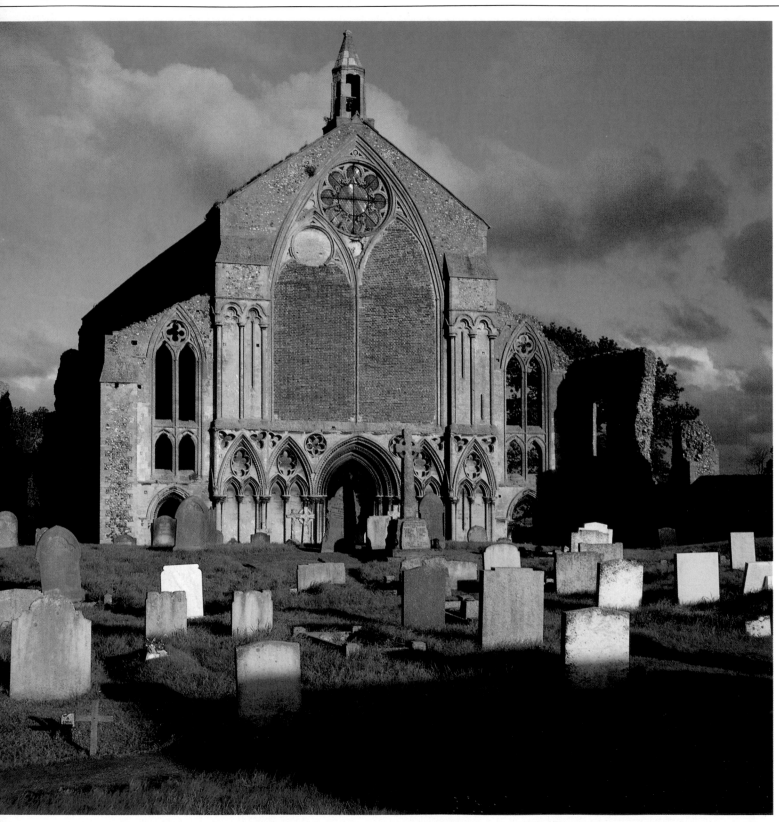

Left:
St Mary's Church, Binham, Norfolk

The presence of the shrine at Walsingham and its great attraction to pilgrims from all over Europe led to the proliferation of abbeys and priories along the various pilgrims' ways across Norfolk. One of these is Binham Priory on the coast road to Blakeney, which was founded c1091, an offshoot of the Benedictine Abbey at St Albans. The largest surviving part of the priory is this church, now the parish church of Binham and standing amid the priory ruins. Despite its rather unsightly bricking up, the west front shown here is of surprising architectural importance. Believed to date from before 1244, it is probably the first native example of the 'Early English' Gothic style — tall narrow windows with pointed arches (earlier Norman arches were all rounded) with what is called 'bar-tracery' at the heads of the individual lancets — and even earlier than Westminster Abbey. This suggests that Binham may have been of sufficient importance to attract highly skilled craftsmen from France, and this again reflects the importance of the Walsingham shrine in the Middle Ages.

Right:
Blakeney, Norfolk

An odd quirk of the tidal flow along the north Norfolk shore has created Blakeney Point — a complex of salt marsh, mud-flats, sand dunes and shingle banks that has been a paradise for bird-watchers and botanists for generations. (It has been owned by the National Trust since 1912.) The same spit protects the pleasant little harbour of Blakeney and makes it nowadays an ideal centre for sailing. In earlier times it flourished as a port for the prolific coastal trade and was important enough in the 16th century to have sent three ships to fight the Spanish Armada. More than 250 species of bird have been sighted near the Point, and varieties scarce elsewhere in Britain — long-tailed ducks, wrynecks, bluethroats and Lapland buntings — are seen each year. Adjoining areas to Blakeney Point acquired by the Trust include Salthouse Broad and Arnold's Marsh, which with its salt lagoons attracts a large variety of waders including avocets. It is administered for the Trust by the Norfolk Naturalists' Trust.

Left:

Burnham Overy Staithe, Norfolk

There is a group of villages in the northwest corner of Norfolk called the Burnhams — once seven in number. The best known is Burnham Thorpe because the now-demolished parsonage there was the birthplace of Admiral Lord Nelson. The biggest is Burnham Market and perhaps the most interesting in Burnham Overy, a village clustering around a maltings, a windmill and a watermill. The Old English word 'staithe' means a landing place and this muddy little harbour once served the millers. Like most places on the East Anglian coast, all is transformed when the tide is in!

Right:

West Runton, near Cromer, Norfolk

What the sea gives to one place, it takes back at another only a few miles down the coast. Here at West Runton the sea helps itself to the soft crumbling sandy cliffs, groynes and breakwaters only slowing the process a little. In some places on the coast of Norfolk it is estimated that a metre of land is lost every year and since Roman times the sea has advanced by over three miles. Farms, cottages, churches and whole villages have vanished under the waves. In this area, for example, at very low tides the stumps of a submerged forest can sometimes be seen and there are traces of a lost harbour. Curiously, however, on balance more land is gained by reclamation each year than is lost by erosion — small comfort to cliff-top dwellers in this area.

Left:

Felbrigg Hall, near Cromer, Norfolk

The present Felbrigg Hall was built for the Windham family — their name derives from Wymondham — about 1620, and was enlarged in 1674-87 and again in 1750. Facing us is the south range, which was the typically Jacobean original in flint, brick and stone — notice the shaped gables, the large windowed bays, the classical decoration around the entrance, the polygonal star-topped chimney stacks and the words *Gloria Deo in Excelsis* cut out of the parapets. The brick west wing on the left was added in 1665, a sedate design in the classical style attributed to William Samwell, a local gentleman architect. It has a hipped roof with dormers, brick quoins and small pediments over two glass doors. The windows are sashed. Internally the house was refurbished in contemporary taste in 1750 after William Windham II returned from the Grand Tour with a number of acquisitions. The architect was James Paine (1717-89) with Thomas Rose, a superb craftsman in stucco and plasterwork. The service range to the right of the south wing may be Paine's work. The house was left to the National Trust in 1970 and is open to the public.

Right:

The Lighthouse, Happisburgh, Norfolk

Corn and kale growing up to the cliff-top lighthouse is a reminder of how fertile the loamy soil is on this lonely corner of northeast Norfolk. Now fully automatic and unmanned, the lighthouse, which was built in 1791, is a good seamark by day and night; and with its namesake, the more readily-pronounced 'Haisborough' lightship offshore, it helps to keep ships out of the treacherous shallows of the Norfolk coast. Daniel Defoe, writing of his great tour in 1724, says, 'As I went by land from Yarmouth northwestwards . . . I was surprised to see that the farmers and country people had scarce a barn or a shed or a stable . . . but what was built of old planks, beams and wales, etc, the wreck of ships, the ruin of mariners and merchants' failures.' In the churchyard at Happisburgh are many sailors' graves, some quite recent, others ancient, some named, others 'known only to God'; most are marked by simple stones, but there is one large unmarked mound to the northwest of the church. It is said to contain the remains of 119 members of the crew of HMS *Invincible* wrecked on Haisborough Sands on 13 March 1801.

Left:

Cottage at Hoveton, Norfolk

Hoveton gives its name to two 'broads' along the
River Bure, northeast of Norwich. It also has two
halls, one c1700, the other c1800, and also a fine
Dutch-gabled Stuart house dating from the end
of the 17th century. This cottage is of the same
period and from its style was obviously the
residence of someone of importance. It has
shaped gables, brick quoins and, of particular
interest, a wide doorway with brick pilasters
supporting a segmental pediment. Part of the
roof is plain tiles, the other of reed thatch.
Weatherings on the chimney stack suggest both
parts were once thatched.

Right:

Blickling Hall, near Aylsham, Norfolk

One of the last of the great Jacobean 'prodigy'
houses, Blickling was built between 1616 and
1627 as fashion was already changing: Inigo
Jones had begun building the Palladian-style
Classical Queen's House in 1616. The master
builder and 'architect' — the word too was new
then — was Robert Lyminge (d1628) who had
also built Hatfield House 12 years earlier. The
long east front seen here has corner turrets with
ogee caps, square and canted bay windows and
shaped gables with finials — English rather than
Netherlandish. In fact the whole exterior owes
little to Classical influence and even the little
pediments over some windows may have been
added in the 18th century when the house was
altered. The interior is almost all Georgian but
the Jacobean long gallery with its exquisite
plaster panelled ceiling survives. The formal
gardens seen here date from before 1729, but the
main parterre and lawns were laid out in 1932. In
the Park the lake was enlarged in the late
18th century: it is a mile long and crescent-
shaped as part of a series of alterations carried
out by John Adey Repton, son of Humphrey
Repton. The house is surrounded by a dry moat
which may have survived from a previous
Blickling Hall, the home of Anne Boleyn,
Henry VIII's ill-fated second wife who was
beheaded on 19 May 1536. Her headless ghost is
said to appear annually on the anniversary of her
execution. The National Trust, which has had the
house since 1940, has no record of anyone ever
seeing her, although the house is open to the
public.

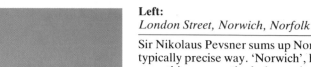

Left:

London Street, Norwich, Norfolk

Sir Nikolaus Pevsner sums up Norwich in his typically precise way. 'Norwich', he says, 'has everything — a cathedral, a major castle on a mound in the middle, walls and towers, an undisturbed medieval centre with winding streets and alleys, 32 parish churches . . .' Originally a Saxon settlement, it became the capital of Norfolk and the main market town for East Anglia. By the Middle Ages it was the third city in England after York and London. Though it may no longer rank so high in size and population its qualities and amenities make it one of Britain's most attractive places to live. Until the end of the 18th century, London Street was known as Cockey Lane, but as local historian Bernard Dorman suggests, the name was changed to give it a London-like quality to attract the best shops. Today it is very much Norwich's 'Bond Street' as the shop fronts here demonstrate with a Regency neo-Classical flavour — contrast it with Elm Hill (page 64). It is now a pedestrian precinct.

Right:

St Ethelbert's Gate, Norwich, Norfolk

The Great or Ethelbert Gate commands one of the entrances to Norwich's attractive cathedral close. It is dedicated to St Ethelbert, king of the East Angles, who was murdered in 794. The gate was built in 1316 by the townspeople of Norwich, it is said, to make amends for riots in the previous century. The elaboration of the niches and the top are characteristic of the 'decorated' style of Gothic although the top was restored by William Wilkins in the 19th century. The house on the right with its Tuscan portico is typical of the many solid red brick Georgian houses to be found in Norwich.

Left:
Elm Hill, Norwich, Norfolk

Give or take a few Georgian doorcases and house fronts — to say nothing of open drains — Elm Street offers a glimpse backwards into the Norwich of medieval and Tudor times when weavers worked behind their looms in the big-windowed attics. The plastering and colour-wash now obscuring the timber framing of the jettied houses probably dates from the 17th century as do the pantiles. It is by no means a contrived street, despite its cobble stones and its overhanging jetties, but one that still houses a variety of crafts.

Right:
Lower Cathedral Close, Norwich, Norfolk

Norwich's cathedral close is divided into Upper and Lower parts and this is the north side of the Lower. The houses here are of varying materials and dates. The house on the left is probably 17th century and in flint rubble although the fenestration seems to be 18th century; the next house on the left (No 50) is again 17th century and is timber framed and plastered with a three-storey porch which now has the ground floor open and four tuscan columns — no doubt thought very fashionable when jetties were out of favour.

Left:

Market Place, Norwich

Norwich market was established by the Normans in 1066 and is open six days of the week. Sir Nikolaus Pevsner says 'It is exactly as a child pictures it, large, full of booths with the proud parish church on one side and the old-fashioned Guildhall on the other, and the proud modern city hall on the third'. The 'old-fashioned Guild Hall' is in the background of this photograph. The older part — on the left — dates from 1407-13 and the newer council chamber on the right from 1535. It is of traditional Norfolk knapped flint with flushwork. The pretty but out-of-character turret was added in 1850. The Guildhall is now used as a magistrates court.

Right:

Loddon House, Loddon, Norfolk

An absolute gem of a 'Queen Anne' house built c1711 although the colour scheme smacks more of the Regency but is probably a modern indulgence. The original house is the five-bay centre, while the piece on the left is a later addition. Of interest are the quoins which give emphasis to the whole façade, especially the three centre bays which have the additional storey with the middle arched window reaching up into the broken bed pediment. The doorcase has Corinthian columns and an open segmented scroll pediment.

Left:
The Chain Ferry, Reedham, Norfolk

The valley of the Yare between Norwich and Yarmouth floods easily and is not well served with bridges, forming a major barrier to traffic moving north and south away from the coast road. At one time it had numerous ferries but this chain ferry at Reedham on the B1140 is now the sole survivor. It carries both cars and people from 8am to 10pm and is not only useful in saving time, but it operates in a most picturesque setting. Just visible behind the ferry is the Ferryboat Inn.

Right:
Yachts on the River Yare near Bramerton, Norfolk

The River Yare is tidal as far as the centre of Norwich and has very few bridges, which makes it both a useful highway for commerce and an interesting extension of the Broads sailing area. Besides the local Broads type of sailing boat, many offshore cruisers find a deep incursion into the countryside of Norfolk a welcome diversion from the chilly rigours of the grey North Sea. Several of the yachts seen here are 'dressed overall' or in 'rainbow fashion', an old custom of celebrating some national, local or private occasion — like the Queen's Birthday — or even the owner's wife's. The flags used are those of the International Code — the successors of those that one of Norfolk's heroic sons once used to tell his Fleet that 'England expects every man will do his duty'.

Left:

South Quay, Great Yarmouth, Norfolk

Said by no less an authority than Daniel Defoe in his *Tour thro' the whole Island of Great Britain* (1724-27) to be the finest quay in England, South Quay has a splendid sequence of Queen Anne and Georgian houses. Many of them would have been new when Defoe first saw them: the first house on the left is dated c1700, for example. In fact some of them go back to the Elizabethan era, have panelled Jacobean rooms and would have been refronted when timber framing became unfashionable. The sea-cadet sail training brig appears to be a visitor and gives a charming 19th century touch to the scene.

Right:

Town Wall and Gate, Great Yarmouth, Norfolk

Medieval Yarmouth was walled on three sides with only the river side open. As it is now, it was long and narrow and only about a mile-and-a-half round its walls. These walls, a random rubble of flint and stone, were built from 1260 onwards and completed in the 14th century. They were over 23ft (7m) high and had 16 towers and 10 gates. The walls enclosed the town until the 17th century and long stretches remain.

Left:

St Nicholas's Church and Vicarage, Great Yarmouth, Norfolk

Yarmouth's parish church has the distinction of being one of the biggest in the country. Like so many large churches in East Anglia it was formerly part of a Benedictine Abbey and was founded in 1101. The present church was dedicated in 1286 but it became ruinous after the Dissolution and was restored c1862 by the Victorians, who among other things put the parapet and the pinnacles on the tower. The church was burned out in an air raid in 1942 and rebuilt in 20th century Gothic. In contrast is the vicarage on the right. The original house, with its two-and-a-half storeys, its slim windows and even slimmer doorway, was built in 1718 — a good example of the best style of Queen Anne or Wren house. The house was extended towards the church in 1781 and the Victorians added the large single storey bay window — but happily, not in Gothic.

Right:

The Mere, Diss, Norfolk

One of the legacies of the last Ice Age is the prevalence of flooded hollows called meres in southwest Norfolk: the one shown here is six acres in extent and the middle of this attractive ancient market town. The flint church in the background is St Mary's, whose tower dates from c1300; much of the rest of the church was somewhat over-restored in the 19th century. Diss has an interesting selection of timber-framed and Georgian buildings, to some of which there seems to have been added a little touch of modern local colour.

Left:
The Scole Inn, Scole near Diss, Norfolk

Formerly the White Hart Inn — the hanging sign still sports a hart — the Scole Inn is a remarkably well preserved Jacobean building dating itself from 1655, the time of the Commonwealth and an odd time for the building of such an ambitious house. Of particular interest are the gables — five of them, each with a pediment, three straight, two segmented — usually known as Dutch and certainly of Netherlandish origin, rather like those on the stables at Blickling which date from 1624. Set halfway between Norwich and Ipswich, the Scole Inn has had a long history as a staging post. Its massive Jacobean staircase has a gate — put in, it is said, to stop travellers riding their horses upstairs.

Right:
St Peter & St Paul, East Harling, Norfolk

A quite spectacular church for a small village, it mostly dates from c1300 and the 'decorated' period. The nave with its superb hammer-beams is 15th century as is the crown of flying buttresses and the spire on the tower.

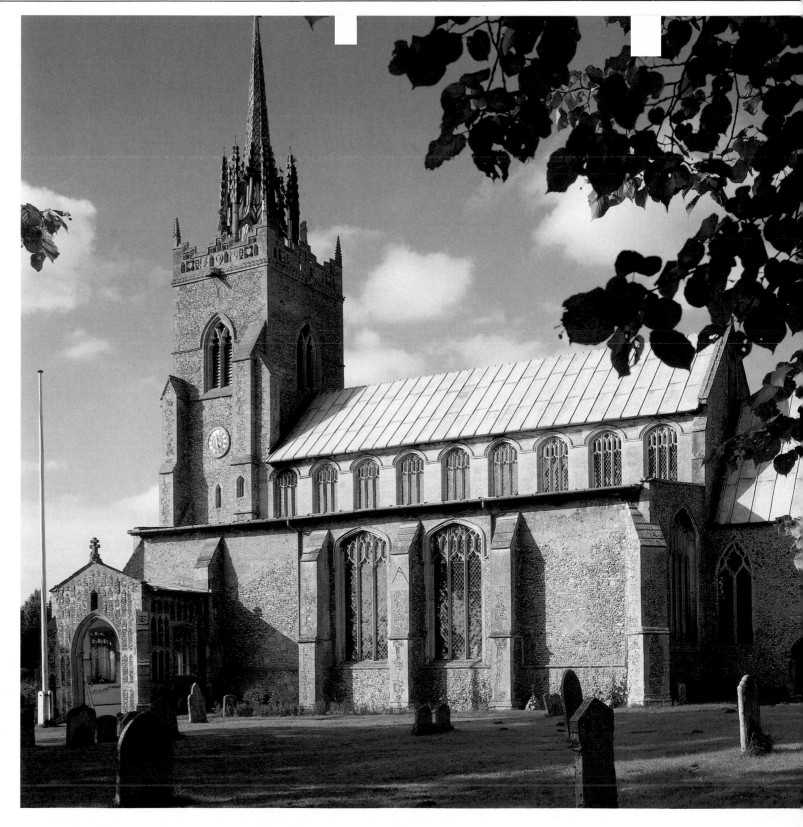

Thetford is the capital of Norfolk's Breckland, and was once set amid the sort of desolate unfarmed heathland that 'Old Crome' loved to paint and the site of the prehistoric flint mines of Grimes' Graves. Thetford Chase now boasts over 52,000 acres (21,000 hectares) of forest land created by the Forestry Commission since 1922. Most of the planted forest is, inevitably, coniferous — Scots and Corsican pine — but there are also stands of beech, oak and chestnut. Roe, red and fallow deer live in the forest and the increasingly rare native red squirrel still survives in the pine forest. Thetford itself stands at the junction of many of the main routes through East Anglia, rivers as well as roads, and at one time was the seat of the Saxon East Anglian kings. Later it had the cathedral of East Anglia but after the Dissolution in 1539 it lost its importance and reverted to being a pleasant and quiet country town. When the passion for spas was at its height c1820 an attempt was made to turn Thetford into an East Anglian version of Cheltenham, but only a heritage of good Georgian houses — and a small pump house — remain.

The statue in front of the flint church is of Thomas Paine (1737-1809), the 18th century radical and renegade whose most famous book, *The Rights of Man* (1790-92), endeared him to the revolutionaries in France but had him indicted for treason at home. He fled to France, only to be saved from the guillotine by the sudden fall of Robespierre. He died in America, there too out of favour with the former revolutionaries. His bones were brought back to England by William Cobbett (he of *Rural Rides*) about 1819, but have since disappeared. They are said to have been buried in Normandy.

Right:

Bishop Bonner's Cottages, East Dereham, Norfolk

Carrying the date 1502, this timber-framed and thatched house was the home of Edmund Bonner, the rector of St Nicholas's — the church in the background — in 1534. He was made Bishop of London in 1540 but lost his post after the separation from Rome. Reinstated during Mary Tudor's infamous reign, he was said to have been a notoriously cruel enforcer of the laws governing heresy and to have sent many Protestants to the stake both in London and in East Anglia. Modern historians however tend to believe that much of his alleged cruelty as related by Foxe in his famous *Book of Martyrs* is exaggerated. Bonner died in prison in Elizabeth I's reign, still refusing to deny Rome.

Left:
Downham Market, Norfolk

Its name tells much of its story — a Saxon
settlement (ham) on a down or hill with a market
. . . But in west Norfolk on the edge of the Fens,
fifty feet makes a hill and for centuries this would
have been a dry spot in a very wet area. In
sparsely populated Norfolk, market towns are of
great importance not only as centres of trade for
local products but as providers of legal, medical,
social and cultural services of all kinds to very
large areas. This is the case with Downham which
serves one of the richest and most productive
agricultural and horticultural regions in the
country, renowned for its fruit and its flowers. A
very busy little town it once stood at the junction
of the A10 from Cambridge to King's Lynn and
the old Roman road from Norwich but is now
by-passed. There is much archaeological
evidence of Romano-British settlements locally
but Downham has little to offer in the way of
historic buildings unless you count this charming
little clock tower. It was built of cast-iron in 1878
by William Cunliffe and the style is unmistakably
Victorian Gothic.

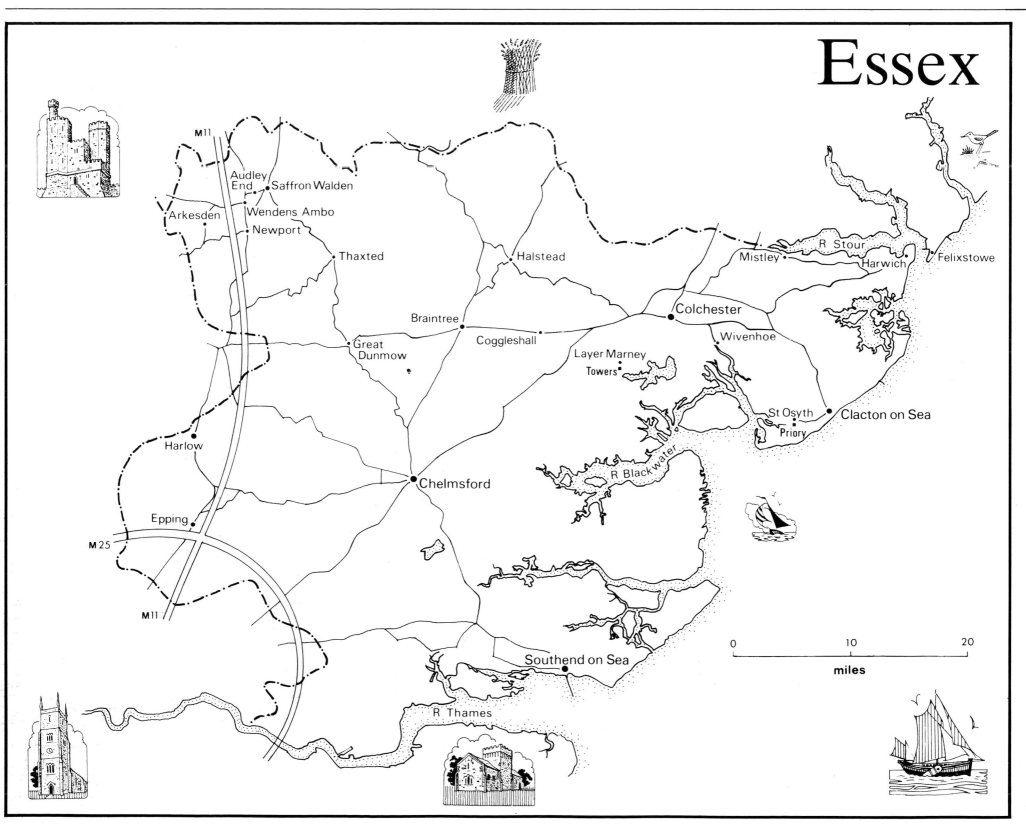

Essex

M11

Audley End
Saffron Walden
Arkesden
Wendens Ambo
Newport
Thaxted
Halstead
Mistley
R Stour
Harwich
Felixstowe
Colchester
Braintree
Coggleshall
Wivenhoe
Great Dunmow
Layer Marney Towers
St Osyth
Clacton on Sea
Priory
Harlow
R Blackwater
Chelmsford
Epping
M25
M11
Southend on Sea
R Thames

0   10   20
miles

Left:

Audley End, near Saffron Walden, Essex

In its day the largest and the most magnificent of all the great Jacobean 'prodigy' houses (see also Blickling Hall, page 61), Audley End was begun in 1603 for the first Earl of Suffolk on what had been the site of the Benedictine Abbey of Walden. When it was built, James I said it was too big for a king but not for his Lord Treasurer. It is now only a fraction of its former size. Sir John Vanbrugh, architect of Blenheim and Castle Howard, worked on the house c1721 and demolished part of it and more was demolished later in the same century. Nonetheless what remains is still on the scale of Hatfield or Blickling but unlike those houses is built of stone not brick. Seen here is the surviving Jacobean façade with its two entrances planned, it is said, one for the king, the other for the queen. (Prodigy houses were built to impress and entertain the monarchy.) Architecturally, the interest is in the symmetry of the façade, the evenness of the fenestration and the two porches. These latter are showpieces as they were meant to be, a fascinating and overcrowded mixture of Elizabethan strapwork and renaissance columns. Internally, besides the surviving Jacobean great hall, there are rooms by Robert Adam.

Audley End is now controlled by English Heritage and is open to the public.

Right:

St Mary the Virgin, Saffron Walden, Essex

This is one of Essex's bigger parish churches and was entirely rebuilt c1450-1525, comparatively late in the Gothic period when the prevailing style was what later came to be called perpendicular. The fullest expression of this particular style is King's College Chapel in Cambridge which was building over a similar period and with which some connections are apparent. The main aspects of the style are readily visible — the tall west tower with its set-back buttresses, its decorated battlements and its big panelled pinnacles; the aisles and the nave are also battlemented and pinnacled and the windows have tall narrow reticulated panels. Of interest is the crocketed spire with its dormers. This was added in 1831 and one of the architects was Thomas Rickman (1776-1841), the man who actually defined the styles of Gothic architecture we still use — Early English, Decorated and Perpendicular. This perhaps explains why his steeple fits in so well. The cottages on the left are timber-framed and jettied and were once thatched. They date from the 16th century and were then probably one building.

Left:

The Old Sun Inn, Saffron Walden, Essex

One of a row of four well preserved 14th and 15th century timber-framed and jettied houses with all the trimmings of East Anglian timber and plaster decoration — curved brackets, carved bressumer and elaborate pargeting — the former Sun Inn carries the date of 1676 in the left-hand gable. This refers to the pargeting and not to the house itself, which must have been around 200 years old when the pargeting was done. The motif in the other gable is an interesting one — that of a pervasive East Anglian legend of Tom Hickathrift and the Wisbech Giant. Tom was himself seven feet tall and was born in the reign of William the Conqueror. Working for a brewer, it was his job to take a dray from King's Lynn to Wisbech through the Fens; one day he was challenged by a giant who had been terrifying the neighbourhood for years. They fought and Tom killed the giant, becoming both rich on the giant's treasure and a hero throughout East Anglia. Ever after he was known not as Tom but as *Mr* Thomas Hickathrift. The Sun Inn was the headquarters of Cromwell and his general, Fairfax, in 1647. It was acquired by the National Trust in 1933 but is let on a long lease as an antique shop.

Right:

Castle Street, Saffron Walden, Essex

As many field names hereabouts reveal, peasants in the Middle Ages grew crocuses to produce saffron, which was used then more as a stimulant than a dye or flavouring. Some 4,000 crocuses were needed to produce a single ounce of saffron and its production was a sizeable industry. Hence the first half of the name of this ancient market town. (The second half is often found in East Anglia — it means the 'valley of the Britons' in Old English — and is derived from the same word as for 'Wales'.) These cheerful jettied cottages along Castle Street date from the 16th century and have had their windows changed over the years. In earlier times they might have been limewashed, sometimes perhaps with a touch of saffron — the buffs, oranges and yellows with occasional pinks. Modern colours certainly brighten the scene.

Left:

Wendens Ambo, Essex

Another village off the M11 and close to the western border of Essex, Wendens Ambo boasts a 'Hertfordshire Spike' on the top of its church tower. Its unusual name derives from Wenden meaning a winding stream, and Ambo simply means that Great and Little Wenden were joined, in the 17th century. The cottages on the left have been well preserved in the plaster and wash vernacular tradition of the area.

Right:

Monk's Barn, Newport, Essex

A much earlier house than the pargeted Crown House that can be seen a little way up the street is Monk's Barn. The presence of a priory here — or perhaps a grange — explains the 'monks', but this building seems unlikely ever to have been a barn. It is a familiar type of 15th century timber-framed yeoman's house known as a wealden house — so-called because it is found most commonly in the area of Kent and Sussex. It comprises a great hall flanked by two jettied wings that have the service rooms at one end and the parlour and solar at the other. The important characteristic is that this is all under a single roof; the wall plate runs across the recessed front, supported by brackets; and, as in this case, has rounded coving. The interesting feature is the oriel window with its carved bracket which is probably a later addition of the early 16th century.

Left:

Clarance House, Thaxted, Essex

Another small East Anglian town that declined in importance with the demise of the wool trade, Thaxted has a range of attractive buildings of various dates. Two of them are here. The post office on the right is probably timber framed, and, by the shape of its roof must, like the rest of Thaxted, once have been thatched. Clarance House is a superb example of the Queen Anne or Wren town house — squarish, red brick, two-and-a-half storeys over a basement, round-headed windows with prominent keystones, and a classical doorcase with a segmental pediment on Corinthian columns. Notice the parapet and the dormers with alternate segmental and triangular pediments. The dormer windows are also casements whilst the rest are sash. The date on the rainwater heads is 1718 but following subsidence the front was rebuilt in its original form in 1951.

Right:

The Guildhall, Thaxted, Essex

Although many medieval Essex towns and churches were built on the profits of the wool trade — or from selling saffron — Thaxted's early prosperity came from making knives, sickles and swords. The cutlers built the church and in 1475 they built this Guildhall. It comprises two jettied stories over an open ground floor that once housed the market house. The double-hipped roof is unusual but the arrangement of the timbers on the upper storey suggest that it is original and divided into two. The steepness of the roof also suggests that it would have been thatched. It has been restored several times over the centuries. In 1714 the naked timbers of the first floor were apparently bricked over and pargeted but in 1911 the plaster and brick were removed, and the timbers were exposed again and darkened to meet the current taste for black and white timber framing. A further restoration in 1976 brought the building more nearly to its likely medieval appearance.

The church of St John the Baptist, just visible here up the hill, is one of the biggest in the county and has been called the 'Cathedral of Essex'. It was built between 1340 and 1510 when the cutlers were prospering, and, as its soaring spire and battlemented and pinnacled tower proclaim, is in the perpendicular style of English Gothic.

Left:
Great Dunmow, Essex

The name of Dunmow is inevitably equated with that medieval precursor of the modern-day TV quiz game, the Great Dunmow Flitch Trial. About every four years married couples volunteering from round about are invited to prove to a local court 'that they have not repented of their marriage for a year and a day' — that is, they have not had a row for a year. If they succeed they are rewarded with a flitch (a whole side) of bacon. The custom is in fact much older than most people realise: it is said to have begun in 1111 and been restored in the reign of Henry III in 1244. In those days aspiring couples had to kneel on sharp stones throughout their ordeal and only eight were successful between 1244 and 1772. Great Dunmow has the usual pleasing selection of plastered buildings of various periods. Seen here is an early 18th century house followed by a Georgian front, and further down are the jetties of a 16th century building. As happens all over East Anglia, many of these buildings are probably timber framed of 16th century date, refronted in later periods to stay in fashion.

Right:
Cottage at Arkesden, Essex

Arkesden stands in a winding valley just off the M11 on the border with Hertfordshire. Besides its ancient church, it is known for its many old cottages. The one seen here is a typical example: it is one-and-a-half storeys high and appears once to have been two semi-detached cottages on slightly different levels. The plaster and colour-wash is in keeping with East Anglian tradition; and from simply looking at it, it is impossible to tell whether it is timber framed or of brick. (It is unlikely to be of clay-lump in this part of Essex.) The thatched roof has gables and is not hipped, again a characteristic of the south of the region — and in no way detracting from the charm of a genuine English country cottage in a genuine English setting.

Left:
Courtauld's Weaving Mill, Halstead, Essex

As the wool trade virtually died out in Essex during the Napoleonic Wars, the descendants of a Huguenot family, the Courtaulds, brought in the silk trade. This Essex family firm was created in 1816 when Samuel Courtauld set up a silk mill at Bocking near Braintree and in 1825 converted this water-powered corn mill on the River Colne at Halstead to producing silk. It was built late in the 18th century and is a most attractive example of the technique of weatherboarding for which Essex is well known. This refined form of overlapping boarding is rather like clinker building in boats with the lower edge of each board chamfered and the upper edge feathered. It required imported softwood from Scandinavia and came into wide use in the southern counties in the late Georgian period when oak was at a premium. Other points of interest are the impressive bands of windows on the first two floors and the wooden shingles on the roof — a perfect counterpart to the weatherboarding.

Right:
Wivenhoe, Essex

A centre for ship and boat-building, exploring the 'magic of the swatchways' or sampling the gourmet delights of the local oysters, Wivenhoe was once a secondary Cinque Port. Before that, the Romans built villas nearby, for they too liked oysters. The church of St Mary the Virgin in the background is mainly 19th century but has a west tower c1500, damaged, it is said, in the celebrated Essex earthquake of 1884. On the quayside is an interesting collection of houses of various dates and including the Nottage Institute. This was a marine training school founded in 1896 with a bequest from Charles Nottage, a Victorian yacht owner who employed local men as paid hands. It now offers courses to yachtsmen.

Paycocke's House, Coggeshall, Essex

One of the finest examples of timber framing and decorative woodwork to be found anywhere in England, Paycocke's was built about 1500 by Thomas Paycocke, a wealthy cloth merchant. It has been called a pure piece of English native domestic Gothic, without any trace of the influence of the Italian renaissance already sweeping the Continent at the end of the 15th century. It was built at a time when good quality oak was plentiful — hence the close studding (as it is called) which would probably have been infilled originally with the traditional wattle and daub. This was replaced with brick infilling as recently as 1905 and the contrast between the red of the brick and the white of the limed oak is quite attractive and much more authentic in East Anglia than the modern passion for making all timber-framed buildings black and white. The particular appeal of Paycocke's lies in its oriel windows with their decorated sills, and the delicately carved fascia board that covers the ends of the projecting floor joists. It carries the initials and the trade sign of Thomas Paycocke — an ermine's tail — just above the filled-in doorway. The house also has some fine moulded and carved panelling and timberwork inside as well as original fireplaces. The house was given to the National Trust in 1924 and is open to the public.

Right:
Bourne Mill, Colchester, Essex

The curved and stepped gables with their finials and the octagonal chimneys are a give-away here — this was an Elizabethan fun house, 'busie and fantasticall' — long before it became a mill. It clearly shows the Flemish influence of the late 16th century and early 17th century seen elsewhere in East Anglia in places like Blickling Hall. It was built in 1591, probably as a fishing lodge, from material quarried from St John's Abbey in Colchester. The house became a cloth mill in the 17th century and was converted into a flour mill in the early 19th century. It was given to the National Trust in 1936 and was restored in the late 1970s. The adjoining pool is apparently renowned for the size of the pike.

Left:

Castle Keep, Colchester, Essex

Probably, as its modern citizens claim, Colchester is the oldest recorded town in Britain, with a settlement here in the fifth century BC. The Romans arrived in 43AD and established a major colony, building, among other things, a temple to Claudius the god. The Britons under Boudicca destroyed the temple and massacred the inhabitants in 60AD, only to be defeated in their turn. The town was rebuilt and was a flourishing city when the Normans arrived in 1066. They built a castle on top of the old Roman temple to strengthen their defences against the Norsemen in 1085. As there was no local building stone they used the old Roman bricks and septaria nodules — a chalky conglomerate. The keep was a hall-keep like that at Castle Rising in Norfolk and the biggest in Europe in its day, complete with great hall and chapel on the first floor. It was in ruins by the 17th century and used inevitably as a quarry. It was saved however by the mid-18th century passion for the 'picturesque' when the present top structure was added, and it did duty as giant garden folly for the nearby Georgian mansion, Hollytrees. Both now cheerfully serve as museums and are open to the public.

Right:

The Gatehouse, St John's Abbey, Colchester, Essex

A type of decoration quite different from Italian Renaissance terracotta is seen on this 15th century monastery gatehouse — abbots, like lords, loved castellations. It is very much an East Anglian technique known as flushwork which is a mixture of limestone and knapped flint arranged in patterns — shafts, blind arches, crockets and tracery — as can be seen here. The limestone is also cut into shields and other heraldic devices. It is of interest to note too that the decorative work appears only on the outside, the 'worldly' side of the abbey gate.

The abbey of St John the Baptist was a Benedictine house, founded in 1096. At the Dissolution the abbey passed to the Crown and the last abbot was hanged for treason to Henry VIII. The remains of the abbey were eventually sold to the town clerk, a lawyer called John Lucas. His descendant, Sir Charles Lucas, was one of the Royalist commanders when Colchester withstood a siege by the Parliamentarians for three months during the Civil War, and his house in the abbey was a strongpoint. After he surrendered, his house was demolished and he was summarily shot. The gatehouse still has marks from Civil War cannon fire but was allowed to stand.

Left:

St Botolph's Priory, Colchester, Essex

Another casualty of the Civil War siege was the great Norman priory church of St Botolph's whose impressive ruins are seen here. The priory was founded between 1093 and 1100 and was the first British house of the Augustinian Canons — known as the Black Canons from their dress. The church was a massive structure and is built of rubble, making use of the ample Roman brick available in Colchester. Roman brick was also used for dressing the piers and arches. This is the nave of the church, 108ft (33m) long, and the piers are 6ft (2m) in diameter. The absence of any embellishment to the arches or the piers indicates that this would have been a typical early Norman church — austere, severe and disciplined, like the Norman god. It became the parish church after the Dissolution, until its destruction during the siege.

Right:

Mistley Towers, Mistley, Essex

Standing as forlornly as the ruins of any ancient abbey demolished at the Dissolution, these twin Classical towers built in 1776 and by Robert Adam are the survivors of a similar architectural outrage by our Victorian forbears. A plain rectangular Georgian church was built here in 1735 but in 1774, as part of his rather grandiose plans to turn Mistley into a 'spaw' like Bath and Cheltenham, an 18th century entrepreneur, Richard Rigby, engaged the services of Robert Adam. Adam built two gatehouses for the nearby hall and also added these two Classical towers to the 1735 church at either end of the nave. As Nikolaus Pevsner says, 'The result was extremely original and far from religious-looking'. That, no doubt, caused its downfall. When the Gothic Revival was at its height in the mid-19th century, many of its protagonists saw the Classical style as pagan and unsuitable for churches. In their religious zeal in other parts of the country they mutilated many delightful Georgian churches both inside and out, adding totally inappropriate Gothic windows filled with their abominable stained glass. At Mistley they went further and demolished the offending nave entirely and in 1871 built a new church some distance away in the 'middle pointed' Gothic style.

St Osyth's Gatehouse near Clacton-on-Sea, Essex

St Osyth, it appears, was either the daughter or the wife of the first Christian king of the East Saxons. She founded a nunnery and, some accounts say, was murdered by Danish raiders c653. An Augustinian priory was founded here c1127 and became an abbey c1261. It was steadily expanded throughout the Middle Ages and by the 15th century was a wealthy establishment able to indulge in much rebuilding. Little remains of the 12th and 13th century buildings but this 15th century gatehouse and the 16th century front of the 'bishop's lodging' (which the last abbot built for himself c1525) have survived. The gatehouse is another example of the superb flint and limestone flushwork seen at St John's Abbey in Colchester. The panelling, the battlements and the tall slender niches above all three entrances, together with the carvings — St George and the dragon — in the spandrels of the main archway, are all in keeping with the perpendicular style of Gothic. Visible through that archway is the façade of the abbot's lodging with its own three-arch entrance. The centre arch is Tudor in shape and above it is a huge oriel window to the abbot's great hall rebuilt in 1865. The abbey has been in private hands since the Dissolution and is open to the public during the summer.

Right:
Layer Marney Towers, Essex

The long-standing English tradition whereby lords lived in castles persisted for quite some time after the need for domestic fortification had passed. It manifested itself in the early Tudors' love of elaborate brick gatehouses — we find them at Hampton Court, St James's Palace and Oxburgh for example — but Layer Marney dwarfed them all. It was intended for a great mansion of which only the gatehouse and the west wing were completed because both the first and second Lords Marney died within two years of each other in the 1520s. There are four turrets here flanking the gatehouse: the two outer turrets have seven storeys and the inner ones eight. Although the towers have corbels that give the impression of machicolations, the battlements have been replaced by terracotta shells with dolphins; similarly the window heads are also in terracotta with Italian motifs. They are the work of itinerant Italian workers and this was how the ideas of the Renaissance first found their way to England — as decorations on what were essentially Gothic structures. Layer Marney Towers is open to the public on frequent occasions during the summer.

Left:
Maldon, Essex

An ancient fishing port set above the head of the Blackwater estuary, Maldon was the scene of a battle between the Saxons and the Danes in 991AD which is celebrated in an Old English poem. It tells of the heroic struggle of one Ealdorman Brythnoth against the invaders under Alnath, the Saxon chief dying from a wound by a poisoned spear at the hour of victory.

Modern Maldon now a fishing port and sailing centre has a wealth of historic buildings, especially old inns and churches. (The tower with the wooden spire in the background is that of St Mary's which is largely Norman.) In the foreground is a fascinating array of workboats and pleasure craft used in the shallow waters of the estuary and the adjoining swatchways and all designed in the East Coast tradition for ease in taking the ground.

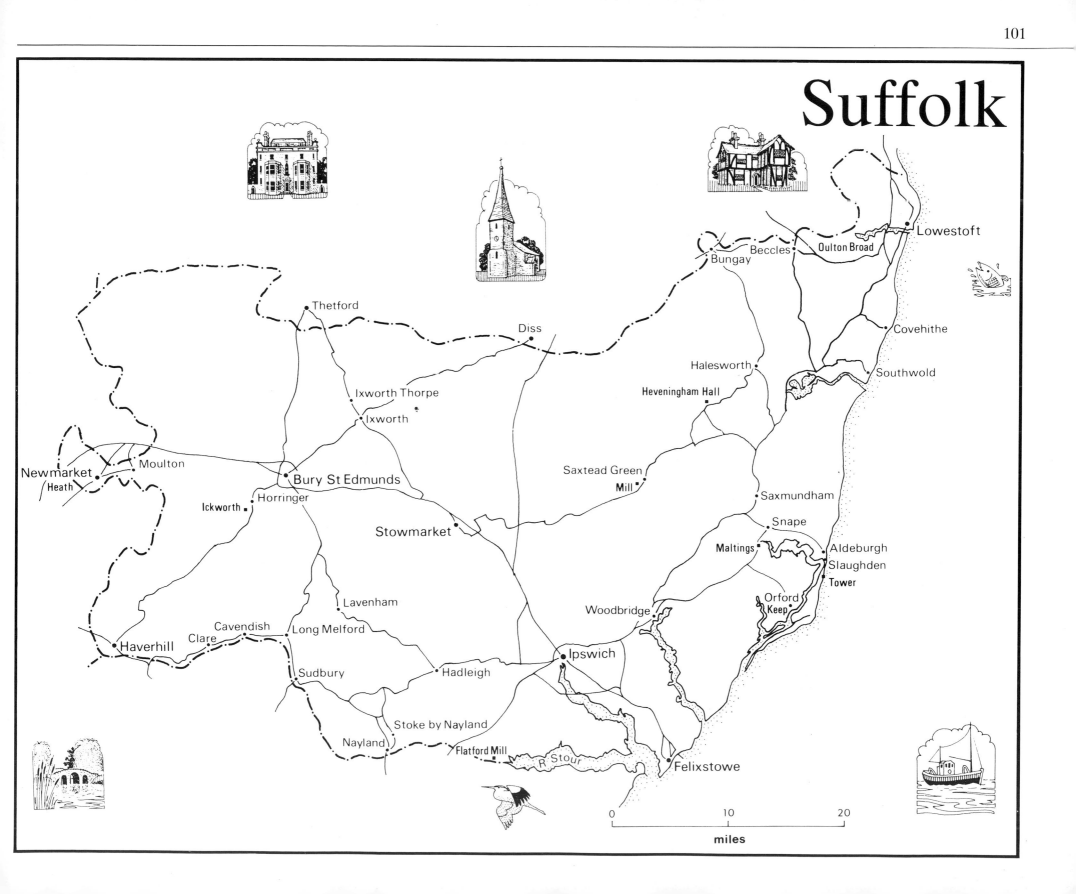

Suffolk

Lowestoft

Beccles • Oulton Broad

Bungay

Covehithe

Thetford

Diss

Halesworth

Southwold

Ixworth Thorpe

Heveningham Hall

Ixworth

Newmarket
Heath

Moulton

Saxtead Green

Mill

Saxmundham

Bury St Edmunds

Ickworth • Horringer

Snape

Maltings

Aldeburgh

Slaughden

Stowmarket

Tower

Lavenham

Orford
Keep

Woodbridge

Cavendish

Long Melford

Clare

Haverhill

Sudbury

Hadleigh

Ipswich

Stoke by Nayland

Nayland

Flatford Mill

R. Stour

Felixstowe

0   10   20

miles

Left:

The Ancient House, Clare, Suffolk

The Ancient House stands in the southwest corner of the great town churchyard of Clare. It is an L-shaped hall house of a style found all over this area for houses of some importance, for example, like that of the local priest. It may well date from the 1493 on the gable end but the pargeting — and the engraved date — are considerably later and the bold naturalistic plasterwork suggests the middle to late 17th century. This form of pargeting is extremely fragile, requiring frequent repairs and renewals. Indeed, the late Alec Clifton Taylor records how he watched skilled workmen from the Ministry of Works replacing, by hand and without moulds, large sections of the shaped plaster. He goes on to tell that a 'fabulous winged monster' below one of the windows had long been lost. The earlier and simpler incised form of pargeting — stick and comb — is seen in the panelling on the gable end.

Right:

Sparrowe's House, Ipswich, Suffolk

Although the quite spectacular pargeting here and the very costly oriel windows all date from the conversion of the house c1670, the alternative name of 'The Ancient House' implies much earlier origins. The existence of a heavy hammerbeam roof of the 15th century confirms that it was originally a medieval timber-framed hall house of the type built by wealthy merchants throughout East Anglia in the late Middle Ages.

This is pargeting on the grand scale — classical pilasters, the coat of arms of Charles II, Neptune, a shepherd and shepherdess, and swags and putti everywhere. Beneath each oriel window, the relief depicts a continent — the most charming is the third from the right, 'Africa', complete with crocodile. The carving of the bressumer ends and the vertical timbers matches the elaboration of the pargeting. Sparrowe's House is now one of the Hatchard bookshops.

Left:
Water Street, Lavenham, Suffolk

Water Street is one of the most rewarding streets in this incomparable small Suffolk town. On the left at the top of the street is the Old Wool Hall, originally a two-storey open hall as its name implies. It probably dates from the early 16th century and its close studding — vertical timbers narrowly apart — is evidence of its importance as a communal building. The jettied overhang on the corner of Lady Street appears to have been filled in with brick. The hall has been part of the Swan Hotel since 1965 and was meticulously restored by the Society for the Protection of Ancient Buildings. On the other corner another jetty has been filled in but the original 15th century shop windows can still be seen fronting on to Lady Street. These would most probably have been cloth merchants' shops and located in their own houses. Jetties have also been filled in on the opposite side of the Water Street but further down one jetty remains and the cheerful pinkish colour-wash is in keeping with East Anglian tradition.

The basis of the national economy in the early Middle Ages was raw wool and East Anglia had the edge over other regions because of its close proximity to Flanders, where most of Europe's cloth was then woven. King Edward III's queen, Philippa, who came from Hainault (now a province of Belgium), gave the cloth trade a tremendous impetus when she brought over the first Flemish weavers to teach their craft to Englishmen. The weavers settled mainly in East Anglia and soon villages in south Suffolk were exporting their products. Some, like Kersey and Lindsey, gave their names to specialist cloth.

Lavenham's pre-eminence in the Suffolk cloth trade in the 15th century owed much to a wealthy clothier, Thomas Spring III, whose memorial is the flushwork panelled south (Spring) chapel of the church. He also provided for the building of the upper half of the magnificent perpendicular tower in his will. His importance to the economic standing of Lavenham went further than that. It is said that in 1524, the year after Spring's death, Lavenham was three times as rich as Long Melford. By 1568 its trade had dwindled to half that of its neighbour.

Right:

Ickworth, Horringer, Suffolk

The builder of Ickworth was one of the more colourful characters of the late 18th century and this remarkable house is a fitting monument to his aspirations and taste. The Hervey family had owned an estate in Ickworth since the Middle Ages and one of them became the first Earl of Bristol at the end of the 17th century. He was succeeded by three of his grandsons in turn and one of them, Frederick Augustus, not expecting to inherit as third son, had already taken orders in the church. He was Bishop of Derry, the richest see in Ireland, when in middle age he became the fourth Earl in 1779, ever after to be known as the 'earl-bishop'. His great love was travelling and the numerous Hotel Bristols throughout Europe owe their name to him. He revelled in all things artistic, collecting old masters wherever he went. His knowledge of classical architecture lies behind the design of this house, which he commissioned from a local architect, Francis Sandys, in 1794. The domed elliptical rotunda seen here was intended to provide the living accommodation, and the quadrant wings and pavilions attached to it to house the earl-bishop's pictures. Unfortunately Napoleon I seized the collection during his Italian campaign in 1798 and the earl died of gout in 1803 when the house was only partly built. It remained untouched until 1821 and not completed until 1829. Even without the earl-bishop's collection, Ickworth contains a marvellous series of family portraits, many old masters — Titian, Velasquez, Hogarth, Reynolds and Gainsborough among them — as well as magnificent silver, ceramics, furniture and books. It was transferred to the National Trust in 1956 and is open to the public.

Left:

Church of the Holy Trinity, Long Melford, Suffolk

This is a splendid village, its long High Street running north and south along a pre-Roman trackway, implying continuous settlement here since Belgic times. Like Lavenham it prospered from the medieval wool trade, and the urge among the wealthy cloth merchants was to buy their way into the next world by generous endowments to the local church in this. The name much in evidence here is Clopton, and there is an impressive Clopton chancery chapel at the east end of the north aisle — appropriately fitted with a fireplace. The church itself is described by Nikolaus Pevsner as 'one of the most moving parish churches of England, large, proud and noble . . .' It was rebuilt on the site of an earlier church c1460-1495 in flint and stone — notice the large areas of sumptuous flush-work — and is a supreme example of the perpendicular style of Gothic. An unusual feature is the three-roofed Lady Chapel which extends the chancel eastwards. It has its own ambulatory. The original brick west tower was replaced as recently as 1903 by the architect G. F. Bodley who has punctiliously maintained the appropriate battlemented, pinnacled and buttressed style of the period to make the whole church as harmonious a building as one could hope to see.

Right:

Church of St Andrew, Covehithe, Suffolk

Covehithe lies on the Suffolk coast between Southwold and Lowestoft and was once a busy port until the sea ate away the soft cliffs and the town began to decline. Of the former village, market place and harbour, nothing remains but the majestic and sad windswept ruins of a great stone, flint and brick church demolished in 1672 after ruination in the Civil War. The 14th century west tower remained in use but was declared redundant in 1974. It now commands no more than a fantastic stretch of clear white sand. The ruins themselves have inspired numerous East Anglian artists, especially those of the Norwich School who loved these desolate places.

The first monastery built on this site, near where the little River Lark is joined by the even smaller River Linnet, was established by Sigeberht, king of the South Landers and patron of St Felix in 630. The place then called Bedericesworth thus became a royal town. Two centuries later, in 869, Edmund, king of the East Angles, a great English patriot and venerated beyond his own kingdom, was murdered by Danish invaders at a place called 'Haeglisdun' — probably present-day Hoxne. When his body was dug up about 30 years later it was found to be uncorrupted, a certain sign of sainthood, and it was transferred to this site which ever since has been known as St Edmundsbury or Bury St Edmunds. In 1020 the Danish King Canute established a small Benedictine monastery here and the Norman kings had it rebuilt on the grand scale between 1090 and 1210 so that it rivalled Ely in size and importance. By the early Middle Ages it had become one of the five richest and most powerful abbeys in England. In 1327 the burghers of Bury rioted against the monastic yoke and destroyed parts of the abbey, and in consequence this mighty gatehouse was built c1330-80 to strengthen its defences. At the Dissolution the abbey was allowed to fall into ruins becoming inevitably a quarry for the town. All that has survived is this gate — the Great Gate — another lesser Norman one and fragments of Norman walling. The Great Gate is built of Barnack stone in the 'decorated' style of English Gothic — pointed arches and niches including ogee shapes, battlements and colonneted buttresses. But in case anyone should get the wrong idea from the peaceful saints standing in their niches in the 15th century, there are the forbidding portcullis and the tactically placed arrow slits as reminders that the abbot had temporal as well as spiritual power.

Right:

Heveningham Hall, Halesworth, Suffolk

The grandest and most elegant 18th century house in Suffolk, Heveningham Hall, was built in 1778 by the architect Sir Robert Taylor (1714-88) for Sir Gerard Vanneck, a London merchant of Dutch descent. The style is that known as Palladian, indicated by the three-storey elevation, the centre-bays embellished by detached 'giant' (covering two storeys) Corinthian columns and the columned and pedimented pavilions at the wings. The rigid Palladian style had dominated English architecture from the 1720s onwards but by this date it was beginning to give way to rather freer interpretations and ideas from other styles. At Heveningham the expected Palladian pediment over the centre is replaced by a heavy 'attic' decorated with statues and relief panels. These are made of Coade stone, a synthetic material that was moulded into classical designs and shapes — including whole statues — at Mrs Eleanor Coade's factory in London.

The design and decoration of the interior was entrusted to James Wyatt, then aged 30, the most fashionable architect of the day and a rival to Robert Adam. At that time he was renowned for his facility with the motives of the 'antique' — the Greek revival and what was known as 'Etruscan', the latter well known even today as the basis of the designs of Wedgwood pottery. The interiors of Heveningham are exquisite. The stucco work, decorative painting and carved fireplaces all drew on the skills of highly proficient artists and craftsmen, many of them brought over from Europe, who at that time travelled the countryside embellishing the country houses of the rich.

Lancelot 'Capability' Brown laid out the grounds here and his plan included the serpentine lake in front of the house. Other features of interest are the orangery which Wyatt also designed and the stables block in the shape of a horseshoe. The kitchen garden also has undulating 'crinkle-crankle' walls which improved the ripening of tender fruit and are said to have been yet another innovation emanating from Holland.

Left:

The Maltings, Snape, Suffolk

Benjamin Britten first came to know this curious landscape in the hinterland of Aldeburgh when he purchased the windmill at Snape and settled here in 1937. It was here at Snape that he wrote his best known opera *Peter Grimes* (1945). He lived in Aldeburgh from 1947 onwards and was the inspiration for the celebrated Aldeburgh music festival whose organising committee commissioned the architects, Arup Associates in the person of David Sugden, to convert this early 19th century maltings into a concert hall in 1966. Further restoration was needed after a disastrous fire in 1969 but despite that the conversion is a masterpiece, preserving externally the more pleasing characteristics of the early industrial building yet at the same time achieving superb acoustics within it.

Right:

Snape Quay, River Alde, Suffolk

This muddy, marshy landscape on the estuary of the Alde, where the gorse shines like gold in early summer, has a past deeply rooted in history. From the sixth century the Saxon Wuffingas made these Suffolk estuaries safe havens for their settlements — the famous Wuffinga ship-burial at nearby Sutton Hoo has tended to overshadow a contemporary one found here at Snape in 1862. In the Middle Ages the priory of Snape controlled all the land around including Aldeburgh, and Snape itself was a flourishing port. Snape Maltings — now, of course, a celebrated concert hall — drew a thriving trade in barley-laden ships and barges throughout the 19th century and the Thames barge seen here is typical of the sort of vessel still employed in the coastal trade. Capable of being handled by a very small crew and of 'taking the ground' without hazard, these fine sailing craft with their high capacity for bulk loads are ideally suited for the task of working the swatchways.

Left:

Tide Mill, Woodbridge, Suffolk

Standing on the banks of the estuary of the River Deben, Woodbridge prospered greatly from wool and shipbuilding in the Middle Ages. It shows its wealth in a legacy of fine buildings which have attracted artists over the generations, John Constable among them. It still retains its maritime character although this is now principally due to its busy yacht marina, boatyards and sailing clubs. The town's great benefactor was an Elizabethan merchant, Thomas Seckford, who not only enlarged the local church, built the grammar school and a row of almshouses, but also donated this Shire Hall built c1575.

First mention of a tide mill at Woodbridge came as early as 1170 and this one was probably first built in the 17th century. It works on the same principle as any water mill except that the tide is used to fill its upper pond, the rise here being about 5ft. The mill has a wheel 20ft (6m) in diameter and 6ft (2m) wide. Once nearly derelict after its main shaft broke, it has been preserved and restored to working order, the only working tide mill in Britain. Alongside it is another splendid specimen of that giant among workboats, the Thames barge with its Dutch sheerline and its lee-boards — a form of offset keel used for working to windward that can be raised in shallow waters.

Right:

Martello Tower, Slaughden, Aldeburgh, Suffolk

Martello towers take their name from their place of origin, a deserted cape in Corsica — actually Mortella — where a small fort with a tiny garrison caused considerable difficulty to the Royal Navy and Royal Marines attacking it in 1794. When Napoleon threatened invasion 10 years later, this design was chosen for a string of towers built by the Royal Engineers along the coasts of Kent, Sussex and Suffolk. There were 74 in all, six of them between the mouths of the Rivers Deben and Ore, standing like sentinels often less than a mile apart. The one seen here is the largest. All the towers were 30-40ft (10m) high and had walls 6ft (2m) thick. There is a gun platform on top, a powder store in the base and the troop quarters on the first floor, entered by ladder through the only entrance, a narrow door 20ft (6m) above the ground. They were never tried in battle but they proved useful in both world wars as observation posts.

Left:
The Keep, Orford Castle, Suffolk

Orford, like Blythburgh, has suffered from the depredations of the sea. This small village was once a thriving port and market town with a royal castle built in the latest mode and an 'Early English' style Gothic church of cathedral proportions. Now the keep of the castle alone remains reasonably intact; of the church, only the roofless choir arcades remain.

The royal castle was built for Henry II in 1165-67 by his 'ingeniator' Alnoth — an architect-cum-master builder — and it was of a revolutionary new design, the first keep in England to have a multi-angled exterior wall instead of a square one. Militarily it was easier to defend without the blind and vulnerable corners of the square type and it also had a curtain wall with rectangular towers that has now vanished. The keep is built of septaria nodules dressed with limestone with a stone base of limestone. It is circular within and has three equally spaced square towers. In one of the towers is a broad staircase; the other two contain chambers. Entrance is on the first floor through a two-storey forebuilding or porch which contains the chapel, while the hall is on the second and third floors of the main building. From the roof one can see the whole coast from Aldeburgh in the north to Bawdsey in the south.

In the middle of the 14th century Orford had a population of around 1,000 and was still thriving in the reign of Elizabeth I when the moorings reached the church along the north side of Quay Street. There were 16 warehouses and at least three inns — the Crown and Castle, the King's Head and the Jolly Sailor — all of which have survived. By the 18th century the river had silted up and the population had declined so that Orford became an infamous parliamentary 'pocket-borough'. It was finally disenfranchised in 1832.

At the beginning of the 13th century Southwold was merely a hamlet attached to Reydon. As the river mouth was opened up by tidal changes in the 15th century it became an influential port, but before the end of the 16th century, the harbour had started to silt up and could only be kept open by digging out the silt to keep the passage clear for shipping. Now the unequal struggle has been almost abandoned and the harbour is used only for small pleasure craft. The 17th century saw an even more devastating event overtake the town when in 1659 it was virtually destroyed by fire — a common fate of timber-framed and thatched towns. It was rebuilt however with many pleasant open greens to diminish the risk of a second fire, with the houses built almost entirely in the local red brick with pantile roofs. This gives the town a distinctly Dutch air, although not long afterwards, in 1672, nearby Sole Bay was the scene of a naval encounter with those same Dutch; nobody won but the weather. That occasion is celebrated in the name of the pub on the right, built a century later. It is a tied house belonging to Adnams, an independent local family brewery with a reputation throughout East Anglia. Behind the pub rises the great white bulk of the lighthouse erected in 1886 on North Green.

Left:

Oulton Broad, Suffolk

In the Middle Ages the Norfolk Broads were formed by the extraction of peat — the exercising of a medieval land right called 'turbary' — which by the 14th century was being carried out on a near industrial scale. That same industry was equally important in this northeast corner of Suffolk. The rent rolls for the two neighbouring parishes show that in the first half of the 14th century the sale of peat provided 76% of the income of Fritton and 31% of that of Flixton, where Oulton was dug. (In the records of the nunnery at Flixton, Bungay, it is recorded for the year 1469 that Thomas Bateman, gentleman, had adopted a new pursuit — the gentle art of angling.)

The peat was not dug out of barren or deserted land: the area was quite populous and in 1066 St Michael's Church at Oulton was among the 10 best endowed in Suffolk. The local saint here was St Felix of Dunwich, a missionary saint who established his see there in 630. The extent of his influence is shown in local names — from Flixton and Friston to Felixstowe in the south. He was buried at Dunwich in 648 but his shrine is at Ramsey Abbey in Cambridgeshire.

Right:

All Saints Church, Ixworth Thorpe, Suffolk

This little village church stands beside Peddar's Way, a prehistoric track which the Romans straightened and improved. It once linked London and Chelmsford to the north Norfolk coast near Hunstanton.

Although the rough-cast render and shingle-hung belfry of the church cannot match the splendours of the great towering flushwork wool churches of Lavenham and Long Melford, it carries its own heritage of faith through the ages. It has a Norman doorway, 'Early English', 'dec' and Tudor windows and diapered brick porch with a Flemish crow stepped gable and flint and brick battlements from the 17th century. Internally the carved poppy heads on the pews show great originality and charm — look out particularly for the mermaid.

Thatched churches are still fairly common in East Anglia but the high price of re-thatching is steadily reducing their numbers. Of 270 recorded in Norfolk at the accession of Queen Victoria in 1837, only about 50 remain. In Suffolk there are about 20 and in the rest of England less than a dozen survive.

Left:

Christchurch Mansion, Ipswich, Suffolk

There was a 12th century Augustinian priory on this site until the Dissolution, and in 1548 a London merchant, Paul Withipoll, bought the lands and the buildings from the Crown. In 1550 he built an 'E-plan' house — central hall with two long projecting wings and a shorter central entrance porch — in the fashion of the time, and similar to other houses in the county, notably Kentwell, Melford Hall and Rushbrooke. The house front of red brick with blue brick diapering and the mullioned and transomed windows on the lower floors are of the Elizabethan period. Queen Elizabeth I stayed in it for six days during her 1561 progress. (It is recorded that she was not best pleased with the entertainment she received.)

Fire destroyed the upper storey of the house in 1674 and it was rebuilt in the Netherlandish style of Blickling earlier in the century — with curved and pedimented Dutch gables. The porch was also remodelled on what passed for modish classical lines at the time but is now known as 'artisan mannerism'. The 'giant' untapered Ionic columns are rather awkward and the balustraded balcony a little out of place.

When Daniel Defoe visited Ipswich in 1722 on his great tour round the island of Great Britain, he commented on the extent to which the park was used by all the townspeople — as crowded as Kensington Gardens, he claimed. As then, so now. Few provincial towns are so fortunate to have such a splendid park and house open for recreation. The house now contains a museum of more than local interest, for, in addition to archaeological remains from the vicinity, and panelling, furniture and ceramics from local houses, it also has several early works by the Suffolk artists Gainsborough and Constable.

Right:

The Gallery, Halesworth, Suffolk

A small market town on the River Blyth some seven miles inland from Southwold, Halesworth has an ancient church that was enlarged in the 15th century when the wool trade flourished and again in the 19th century when the coming of the railways made the town busy and prosperous. This simple brick building close to the church is probably much older than it looks as it is recorded in the 15th century archives. It also once housed immigrant Flemish workers. In the late 17th century it was converted into almshouses — the curved gables indicate the style of the time — and is now the Halesworth Gallery and open to the public in the summer. It also houses the local county library.

Left:

The Beach, Lowestoft, Suffolk

Lowestoft has been a fishing port since the Middle Ages, thriving in the days when the North Sea enjoyed an annual glut of herring. In medieval times the herring were cured by a system of salting and smoking until the proverbial 'red herring' was produced, a source of protein that was impervious to heat or moisture and remained edible for weeks if not months. It was exported all over Europe. (The bloater is its descendant and came into existence in the 17th century, but is a milder cured beast. The kipper only dates from the middle of the last century and is the most delicately cured of the three.) Gross overfishing for fish meal with purse seine nets by the Dutch and Norwegians in the mid-1960s exhausted the herring supplies and the East Anglian herring trade collapsed. A ban on herring fishing was imposed internationally in 1977; and while it is still strictly controlled, shoals have begun to make a recovery.

Lowestoft is also very much a seaside resort with, as is evident here, superb sandy beaches. The area south of the harbour was developed in the mid-19th century with the arrival of the railways (which reached Lowestoft in 1847), the development continuing throughout the 19th century. The hotel on the cliff is the Victoria, opened in 1897.

Right:

Cavendish, Suffolk

The epitome of the East Anglian village green, Cavendish has a flint and limestone church fronted by thatched and colour-washed cottages. The west tower of the church dates from the 14th century and is distinctive because of its prominent stair turret that is higher than the tower itself and carries a triangular bell-cote. Just visible over the cottages is the west end of the south aisle with its flushwork battlements. It dates from the end of the 15th century. The cottages are thatched in Norfolk reed with wheat straw ridges and the thatch comes well down between the dormer windows.

Left:

Newmarket Heath, Suffolk

Public horse races were first held in England during the reign of James I (1603-25), but of the four racecourses established during his reign, only Newmarket survives. The first race was held here in 1605 and from that date it became the headquarters of the Turf. Charles I had other more pressing concerns and Lord Protector Cromwell banned the sport because of 'the evil use made thereof by such ill-disposed persons as watch for opportunities to raise new troubles'. With the restoration of the 'Merry Monarch' in 1660, horse-racing attained a new importance in court life. Sir Christopher Wren remodelled King James's old house at Newmarket to serve as a royal palace. Thereafter the royal interest has continued to the present day. The Jockey Club was founded at Newmarket in 1750 and later the same century the Prince Regent established a royal stud.

Charles II's interest in the sport extended to watching his horses in training and, as we see them here, at their daily gallops. His customary position on top of Warren Hill is still known as the King's Chair. It was however one of the Hanoverians, the Duke of Cumberland, who made the greatest contribution to English pre-eminence in the 'Sport of Kings'. He it was who bred Eclipse, probably the greatest racehorse of all time. It is said that today there is not a single thoroughbred horse in the world that does not bear the blood of Eclipse in its veins. One of those we see here exercising on this famous stretch of East Anglian heath may yet be another Eclipse.

Right:

Moot Hall, Aldeburgh, Suffolk

In the museum in this historic Moot Hall there is an Elizabethan town plan showing how closely the Tudor buildings pressed around it. As a meeting place and market hall it was the centre of the medieval town until the sea gradually eroded it all away, leaving this little building, the sole survivor of its period, standing isolated on its stretch of green sward like the stage set which it has inspired for Benjamin Britten's operas. Modern Aldeburgh is now principally a 19th century town brought into fame and fortune by its celebrated music festival. The Moot Hall itself is timber framed, jettied and close-studded with the carved bressumer fascia board which is typical of East Anglia. It dates from c1530, with its brick nogging about a century later. The brick side-wall and the picturesque chimney stacks which look all of a piece were added only in the 19th century.

Left:

Willy Lott's Cottage, Flatford, Suffolk

'These scenes made me a painter . . .' Although he painted elsewhere in England, John Constable (1776-1837), the son of a wealthy mill-owner, found his real inspiration from the scenes around his father's mill at Flatford. He was particularly devoted to this house on the banks of the tranquil Stour, called Willy Lott's cottage. There is a surprising shock of recognition when the modern visitor first confronts the scene that Constable painted in 'The Haywain' and 'The Mill Cottage' This comes partly from the almost unchanged surroundings but more from Constable's translation of Nature on to canvas in the manner of the great Dutch masters. As he once wrote himself: 'I shall shortly return to Bergholt where I shall make laborious studies from Nature — I shall endeavour to get a pure and unaffected manner of representing the scenes that may employ me . . . There is room enough for a natural painter.'

The National Trust, which has owned both Flatford Mill and Willy Lott's cottage since 1943, is determined to preserve the scenes that Constable depicted. To that end it has recently undertaken the laborious task of raising the old river barge that appears in several of his pictures of this stretch of the Stour. The barge was discovered sunk deep in the mud at the bottom of the river and its raising and restoration has been a fascinating exercise in the field of nautical archaeology.

Right:

Moulton, Suffolk

Moulton lies on the western borders of Suffolk in the region known as 'The Fieldings', so named because long after the rest of Suffolk's open fields had been enclosed, these remained open and strip cultivated. Now bypassed by the A45, the village was formerly a thoroughfare, and the little River Kennet is crossed by two ancient bridges. This one, the more northerly, is a most impressive five-arch bridge built in the 15th century from random flint rubble. Its arches are brick lined.

Bibliography

General

The Pattern of English Building, Alec Clifton Taylor, Faber.

Houses in the Landscape, John & Jane Penoyre, Faber.

The National Trust Guide, R. Fedden — R. Joekes, Cape.

Folklore Myths and Legends of Britain, Reader's Digest.

British Building Styles Recognition, Alan Hollingsworth, Ian Allan Ltd.

Historic Houses, Castles & Gardens Open to the Public, Leisure Publications, 1986.

East Anglia

The Buildings of England, ed Sir Nikolaus Pevsner, Penguin:
Bedfordshire, Peterborough & Huntingdon
Cambridgeshire
Essex
North West & South Norfolk
North East Norfolk & Norwich
Suffolk.

The King's England, Arthur Mee, Hodder & Stoughton:
Bedfordshire & Huntingdon; Norfolk, Essex, Suffolk.

Shell Guide to Norfolk, Wilhelmine Harrod, Faber.

Norfolk, Bernard E. Dorman, Batsford.

Suffolk, Allan Jobson, Hale.

Essex, S. A. Manning, Hale.

The Suffolk Landscape, Norman Scarfe, Hodder & Stoughton.

Suffolk & Norfolk, M. R. James, Dent.

Norwich in Pictures, A. Kent & Bernard E. Dorman, Jarrold.

Index